Foreword

In recent years there have been a number of pieces of legislation which have altered the sentencing framework in England and Wales. In particular, the Criminal Justice Act 1991 (as amended by the Criminal Justice Act 1993) introduced a new framework for sentencing. This research was commissioned to examine current sentencing practice in magistrates' courts and the Crown Court in more detail than that routinely provided by Criminal Statistics.

It combines a survey of 3,000 sentenced cases in 25 magistrates' courts with interviews with 126 magistrates and almost 2,000 sentenced cases in 18 Crown Court centres. Information is provided about factors which influence the sentencing decision and about magistrates' views on the different sentencing options. Possible sources of disparity in sentencing are discussed and changes in sentencing patterns over the past few years are examined.

DAVID MOXON
Crime and Criminal Justice Unit
Research and Statistics Directorate

Acknowledgements

We would like to thank all the magistrates' and justices' clerks who gave up their time to speak to us. Thanks are also due to the court staff who made the team welcome in the 25 magistrates' courts that participated in the survey.

We would also like to thank all those probation officers working in the Crown Court who collected data for taking the time to complete questionnaires in addition to their normal workload.

Many colleagues in the Research and Stastistics Directorate (RSD) provided advice and encouragement: particular thanks to Jennifer Airs, Patrick Collier, Pat Dowdeswell, Robin Elliott, Marian FitzGerald, Carol Hedderman and David Moxon. Margaret Ayres and Ricky Taylor provided additional figures from Criminal Statistics. In magistrates' courts the survey data was collected by Joanna Bartlett, Tamsen Courtenay, Ian Hearden, Hilary Legard, Tiggey May and Jason Preece. In five Crown Court centres the survey data was collected by Hilary Legard, Elizabeth Butler, Ruth Lewis and Nicola Ponikiewski. Ruth Lewis and Nicola Ponikiewski gave invaluable assistance with the data collection, data preparation and early analysis.

CLAIRE FLOOD-PAGE
ALAN MACKIE

Sentencing Practice:
an examination of decisions in magistrates' courts and the Crown Court in the mid–1990's

Claire Flood-Page and Alan Mackie

A Research and Statistics Directorate Report

Home Office
Research and
Statistics
Directorate

London: Home Office

Home Office Research Studies

The Home Office Research Studies are reports on research undertaken by or on behalf of the Home Office. They cover the range of subjects for which the Home Secretary has responsibility. Titles in the series are listed at the back of this report (copies are available from the address on the back cover). Other publications produced by the Research and Statistics Directorate include Research Findings, the Research Bulletin, Statistical Bulletins and Statistical Papers.

The Research and Statistics Directorate

The Directorate consists of Units which deal with research and statistics on Crime and Criminal Justice, Offenders and Corrections, Immigration and General Matters; the Programme Development Unit; the Economics Unit; and the Operational Research Unit.

The Research and Statistics Directorate is an integral part of the Home Office, serving the Ministers and the department itself, its services, Parliament and the public through research, development and statistics. Information and knowledge from these sources informs policy development and the management of programmes; their dissemination improves wider public understanding of matters of Home Office concern.

First published 1998

Application for reproduction should be made to the Information and Publications Group, Room 201, Home Office, 50 Queen Anne's Gate, London SW1H 9AT.

©Crown copyright 1998 ISBN 1 84082 115 9

ISSN 0072 6435

Contents

Summary

This study examined sentencing practice in both magistrates' courts and the Crown Court. It is based on a survey of 3,000 magistrates' courts cases, 1,800 Crown Court cases and Justices Clerks in 12 areas. The main findings were as detailed below.

Factors associated with more severe sentencing at both higher and lower courts

The decision to imprison

- A custodial sentence was more likely if the offender was seen to pose a risk to the public, if the offence was planned or unprovoked, if a serious injury was inflicted or where the victim was especially vulnerable.

- Those with previous convictions, especially for a similar offence, were more likely to get custody.

- An offender who was subject to a court order when they committed the current offence was also more likely to receive a custodial sentence.

Community sentences

- Factors which were important in the custodial decision at the Crown Court often featured in the cases attracting community disposals at magistrates' courts. Thus, for example, in cases involving a breach of trust, magistrates' courts were particularly likely to impose a community penalty whereas at the Crown Court this was more likely to lead to a prison sentence.

- Among those given a community sentence, women were less likely than men to receive a community service order (CSO) or a combination order, and more likely to receive probation.

Financial penalties

- Use of fines continues to fall at both higher and lower courts; they are used most often for first offenders who are in work.

- Use of compensation orders has also fallen substantially in recent years. Often no reason is given in court (though one can often be deduced easily); but there is continuing evidence that the amounts of compensation awarded are less than they should be because sentencers impose a fine or costs as well. There is continuing reluctance to award compensation as a sentence in its own right.

Magistrates' courts

- Among those with previous convictions 4 per cent of females and 16 per cent of males received a custodial sentence.

- Twenty-one per cent of repeat burglars (i.e. offenders with at least one previous conviction for burglary) were given a custodial sentence.

- Combination orders were used more for those with previous convictions and also those convicted of violence and burglary. Probation and combination orders were used for a higher proportion of offenders who were mentally ill or under stress than CSO.

- Stipendary magistrates sentenced a higher proportion of offenders to custody than lay magistrates after allowing for other factors.

- Women were more likely to be given a discharge and less likely to be fined.

- Magistrates all applauded the introduction of the combination order which they saw as the 'helping' role of probation with 'punishment' in the form of community service.

- Magistrates welcomed the opportunity to make additional requirements to probation, enabling them to tailor orders more closely to the offenders' circumstances.

- Attendance centres were rarely used. Not all courts have access to a centre but sometimes practical considerations made it difficult to impose an attendance order. Magistrates were concerned that the activities that offenders took part in were sometimes a soft option, and wanted offenders to do more physically demanding activities.

- Unemployed offenders were twice as likely as employed offenders to receive a conditional discharge. Magistrates said that they would often impose a conditional discharge where they did not believe the offender had the ability to pay a fine.

- Courts used a range of methods to calculate the size of a fine. For example, in some areas magistrates believed that fines should be proportionate to income and so increased fines for high income offenders. In others, magistrates felt that it was wrong to penalise wealthy offenders.

- The main reason for not awarding compensation where there was injury or loss was that the offender did not have enough money to pay. In property offences, magistrates expected to see some evidence of the value of the loss, for example a receipt. Often no evidence was provided or else unverifiable information such as an estimate and in this situation sentencers were reluctant to award compensation.

Crown courts

- Offenders who pleaded guilty had their sentences reduced, on average, by just over a third. Early guilty pleas attracted the greatest discounts.

- The Criminal Justice Act 1991 S2(2)(b) allows longer than normal sentences to be awarded where the offence is a violent or sexual offence in order to protect the public. Longer than normal sentences were awarded in three per cent of violent offences and six per cent of sex offences.

- Sentences were most frequently suspended in cases of fraud and forgery. The commonest reasons for suspense were illness or caring responsibilities.

- Fines were most likely for offenders in work: 10 per cent of employed first offenders were fined compared to two per cent of those without a job. No unemployed offenders with previous convictions were fined but eight per cent of those in work were.

- Many fines would take a long time to pay. For example, the average fine for an unemployed person was £340 which, at the rate of £5 a week, would take 16 months to pay. The maximum amount generally regarded as payable by a person on income support is £5 a week.

- Compensation was awarded in 26 per cent of violent offences not attracting a custodial sentence but only 14 per cent of burglary, ten per cent of fraud and forgery and eight per cent of theft cases.

- The main reason for not awarding compensation where there was injury was that the offender did not have enough money to pay. A common reason for not awarding compensation in injury and property offences was that the victim had not asked for it.

- There was no evidence that black or Asian offenders were more or less likely than whites to receive a custodial sentence when other factors were taken into account.

- Women were less likely than men to receive a prison sentence when other factors were taken into account. Custody was awarded to 42 per cent of women first offenders compared to 49 per cent of men. Among those with previous convictions, 63 per cent of men and 49 per cent of women received a prison sentence. Women were also less likely to be fined than men. Among those who received a community sentence, women offenders were more likely than men to receive probation or a combination order. A smaller proportion of women received a CSO.

Conclusions

- Closer co-operation between sentencers and the probation service could help both to ensure that probation schemes deliver what sentencers require, and that sentencers are aware of what the service can deliver.

- Restoring the use of the fine, which has largely been replaced with expensive alternatives, could enable probation resources to be focused more effectively, with potential benefits to reconviction rates while also regenerating revenue from fines.

- Courts need to be further reminded of the need to give precedence to compensation, and never to reduce compensation for lack of means where they also impose a fine or costs.

- It is worth considering whether the tight restrictions imposed on suspended sentences are still appropriate after the custody threshold was effectively lowered by the Criminal Justice Act, 1993.

- Large disparities in sentencing between courts, revealed by routine statistics, indicates that there is a case for a fresh assessment of what weight should be given to factors in sentencing decisions, and for improving the mechanisms for encouraging consistency. By showing what factors currently influence sentencers, the study will inform future discussion of the issue.

Part I

Sentencing framework and overview of recent trends

Claire Flood-Page

1 Introduction

This chapter provides an overview of the current sentencing framework, and recent trends in sentencing are described in Chapter 2. Part 1 therefore sets the context for the analyses of sentencing in magistrates' courts and the Crown Court, which are presented in Parts 2 and 3.

The sentencing framework

The Criminal Justice Act (CJA) 1991 introduced a legislative framework based primarily on a 'just deserts' approach, but coupled with incapacitation for 'dangerous' offenders. The Act developed the work of the Court of Appeal which had been moving towards sentencing which gave more emphasis to the offence and less to the offender – the 'just deserts' principle (Home Office, 1990). While the seriousness of the offence has always been a key factor in sentencing, the new framework gave it additional weight by setting thresholds for community sentences and custody. At the same time, longer sentences were introduced for those offenders who were convicted of violent or sexual offences and who were considered to be a danger to the public.

In adopting a more desert-based sentencing structure, England and Wales joined a number of other Western countries. For example, Canada, Sweden, Finland, the State of Victoria in Australia and many states in the US moved in this direction during the 1980s and early 1990s. As part of this process, some opted for an increased use of mandatory sentences, others for sentencing guidelines (Morgan and Clarkson, 1995). England and Wales did not adopt either of these approaches; instead the CJA 1991 laid down basic rules for the use of custody, community sentences, fines and discharges (Wasik, 1993) The sentencers occupy levels in a 'pyramid' with custodial sentences at the apex and fines and discharges at the base (Figure 1.1). The concept of the 'seriousness' of the offence is the tool for moving between the bands (Ashworth, 1992).

Figure 1.1: The sentencing framework following the Criminal Justice Acts 1991 and 1993

CUSTODY

Criterion: Offence Seriousness (S. 1(2) (a))
or protection of the public following a violent or sexual offence
(S.1(2) (b))

- Imprisonment (21 and over)

- Detention in a young offender institution (15 - 20)

- Exceptionally, imprisonment (but not youth custody) may be suspended

---

COMMUNITY SENTENCE

Criterion: Offence Seriousness (S.6(1)) and suitability for order
(S.6(1))

- Combination order (16 and over)

- Probation order (additional requirements may be specified) (16 and over)

- Community Service Order (16 and over)

- Supervision Order (additional requirements may be specified) (10-17)

- Attendance Centre Order (under 21)

FINANCIAL PENALTIES

- Fines

- Compensation orders (as a sentence in its own right or with another)

OTHER SENTENCES

- Discharges (Conditional or absolute)

The principal changes made by the CJA 1991, as amended by the CJA 1993 and supplemented by the Criminal Justice and Public Order Act 1994 were:

- Probation became a sentence of the court: previously it was an alternative to sentencing available for any type of offence. In the new framework, probation became a community sentence for offences of intermediate seriousness.

- Community service was established as a sentence in its own right rather than an alternative to custody.

- The combination order was introduced, combining community service and probation. The 1992 Standards for the Supervision of Offenders in the Community stated that this was to be a demanding penalty catering for offenders who might otherwise have received immediate custody.

- The attendance centre order, available only to those aged 21 or under, must be justified with respect to the seriousness of the offence. It seeks to punish through restriction on leisure time; to provide occupation and instruction to assist the development of self-discipline, skills and interest; and develop social skills through structured activity.

- Partly suspended sentences were abolished, which reflected changes that were made to automatic release.

- Restrictions were placed on the use of suspended sentences which could only be used in 'exceptional circumstances'.

- Unit fines were introduced by the CJA 1991, but abandoned in the 1993 Act. However, the later Act did retain elements of the means-based approach to setting fines, in that fines could be increased for the better-off as well as reduced for the poor.

- in considering the seriousness of the case, previous convictions, offending while on bail and the offender's failure to respond to previous sentences could be taken into account.

- The Criminal Justice and Public Order Act 1994 gave legislative force to discounts for guilty pleas, which had long been endorsed by the Court of Appeal. The Act stated that sentencers should take account of the stage in the proceedings at which a guilty plea was entered, but did not specify what the discount might be.

Custody

The threshold criteria for use of custody are:

- The offence, or the offence and one or more offences associated with it, is so serious that only such a sentence can be justified.

- The offence is a sexual or violent offence and only such a sentence would be adequate to protect the public from serious harm from the offender.

- Following refusal to consent to a community sentence which requires such consent (or for serious breach of such a sentence)[1].

There is relatively little formal guidance to help sentencers assess whether a particular offence is 'so serious that only a custodial sentence can be justified' (the 'custody test'). The leading case is Bradbourne (1985)[2] in which a young supermarket cashier pleaded guilty to stealing £2 from the till and received three months detention. In this case, the Court of Appeal held back from defining 'seriousness', but said that the right question for the court to ask in passing a custodial sentence was whether it was:

> the kind of offence which would make a right thinking member of the public, knowing all the facts, feel that justice had not been done by passing any sentence other than a custodial one.

In Cox (1993)[3], L.J. Taylor confirmed that this 'right-thinking persons' test was the correct approach. The seriousness of an offence is therefore a subjective judgement which can differ between individuals and/or over time (Ashworth and Hough, 1996).

Custody is available for indictable and triable-either-way offences and some summary offences. Magistrates' courts may impose custodial sentences of up to six months, or 12 months in aggregate, where there are two or more either-way offences. Where custodial sentences are imposed for more than one offence, the sentences may run either concurrently or consecutively.

---

1   The requirement for consent for community sentences for offences committed after 1 October 1997 has been removed by the Crime (Sentence) Act 1997.
2   Bradbourne (1985) 7 Cr App Rep (S) 180.
3   Cox (1993) 14 Cr App (S) 470.

Suspended sentences

The rationale for the suspended sentence is that the threat of imprisonment will act as a deterrent, and as such it sits uneasily within the desert-based approach of the 1991 Act which imposed major restrictions on its use. Most importantly, a suspended sentence can only be imposed where the custody threshold has been reached. It is not to be seen as an intermediate sentence between custody and community sentences. The Court of Appeal has interpreted the term 'exceptional circumstances' narrowly, and it excludes previous good character, provocation, early guilty plea, etc. Such factors are considered relevant to whether the custody threshold is reached, not to the question of whether it is appropriate to suspend. A suspended sentence is often combined with other sentences, such as a fine or compensation order. It may not be combined with a probation order, although a sentencer may impose a suspended sentence supervision order whereby probation supervision is provided, but these have become extremely rare.

Community sentences

While the CJA 1991 gives guidance on when a community sentence can be imposed, there is little formal guidance for the sentencer on the choice between community sentences. The Court of Appeal has said little about this if only because few people who receive a community penalty appeal against sentence. The *National Standards for the Supervision of Offenders in the Community* (Home Office' 1995), however, gives helpful guidance:

- A probation order aims to secure the rehabilitation of the offender, to protect the public from harm from the offender or to prevent the offender from committing further offences.

- Community service orders (CSOs) are 'to prevent further offending by re-integrating the offender into the community through punishment – by means of positive and demanding work and by keeping to disciplined requirements – and to make reparation to the community by undertaking socially useful work'.

- A combination order has both these aims.

The standard conditions of probation are that the offender keep in touch with the probation officer responsible for his/her supervision in accordance with such instructions as he/she may from time to time be given by that officer and notify him/her of any change of address'.

In addition, the courts may require that during the whole or part of the order, the offender must comply 'with such requirements as the court, with regard to the circumstances of the case, considers desirable' (Powers of the Criminal Courts Act 1973 s3(1)). The type of additional requirement which can be made varies between probation areas, according to what the local probation service has established.

The attendance centre order is also available for offenders under 21.

Compensation orders

Compensation orders were introduced in the Criminal Justice Act 1972 to provide victims with 'a convenient and rapid means of avoiding the expense of resorting to civil litigation when the criminal clearly has the means which would enable the compensation to be paid' (Scarman L.J. in *Inwood* 60 Cr App R 70). As increasing prominence has been given to the interests of victims, successive pieces of legislation have encouraged the use of compensation. The Criminal Justice Act 1988 (section 104(1)) requires a court to give reasons for not awarding compensation and therefore obliges sentencers to consider compensation in every case where there has been loss or damage to property or personal injury. The 1988 Act also extended the scope of the order allowing compensation to be awarded for damage to vehicles or property caused by uninsured vehicles.

The CJA 1991 raised the maximum level of compensation that could be ordered by a magistrates' court in respect of each offence from £2,000 to £5,000 and allowed compensation orders to be deducted directly from an offender's income support. Compensation takes precedence over a fine when the offender does not have the means to pay both.

Guidance for sentencers

There are no formal guidelines for sentencing in England and Wales but there are a number of sources of guidance available to sentencers.

• From time to time the Court of Appeal uses issues raised in individual cases to set out more general guidance for particular offences. For example, in Billam (1985) the court gave guidance on the sentencing of rape; the sentencing of bank robbery was discussed in Daly (1981). These judgements have tended to focus on the most serious cases dealt with at Crown Court, although the Court has more recently turned its attention to some of the more run-of-the-mill cases such as burglary and theft which form the bulk of the workload of the Crown Court.

- Magistrates' Association Sentencing Guidelines cover offences which magistrates deal with regularly in adult courts. They give starting points for different types of offence, and list the kind of aggravating and mitigating factors which might make either a more or less severe sentence appropriate in an individual case. It is stressed that the guidelines are not a tariff, and that the factors listed are not exhaustive. The Guidelines are issued with the blessing of the Lord Chancellor and the Lord Chief Justice, and are endorsed by the Justices' Clerks' Society. Individual courts adapt the Magistrates Association sentencing guidelines as they believe appropriate and so the guidelines in use will differ between areas. The most recent edition was issued in April 1997 and so post-dates the fieldwork for the present study.

- The Sentence of the Court is a handbook for magistrates which is produced under the auspices of the Justices' Clerks' Society and is endorsed by the Lord Chief Justice. It provides a straightforward guide to the role of each sentence and a clear description of the overall sentencing framework. It plays an important part in training, as well as being a reference guide.

The study

Aims

Basic information about trends in sentencing is provided by the annual publication of *Criminal Statistics, England and Wales*. The purpose of the present study was to provide a more detailed account of the way in which magistrates and judges were using the new sentencing framework. Particular questions included:

- What factors make an offence 'so serious' that only a custodial sentence is appropriate?

- When is the power to suspend a custodial sentence used?

- What is the effect of plea on sentence?

- When are community sentences used, and what factors lead to the use of one rather than another?

- When are fines used, and how are they set in relation to income?

- When is compensation awarded, and what reasons are given for not ordering compensation in cases involving injury, loss or damage?

- Do extra-legal factors, notably the ethnic origin or sex of the offender, influence sentences?

- Do stipendiary magistrates sentence differently from their lay colleagues?

- Where guidelines exists, i.e. through the Court of Appeal for some offences and through the Magistrates' Association for a wide range of offences dealt with by the lower courts, how do actual sentences compare?

The data

- Observers in court recorded what was said by the defence and prosecution. This is often the only way to find out what aggravating and mitigating factors were brought to sentencers' attention.

- Court records, including the police antecedents and any pre-sentence report, provided details of criminal history and other background information including employment status, whether the offence was committed while on bail, whether the offender was in breach of another sentence, etc.

- One hundred and twenty-six magistrates and 12 justices' clerks took part in group interviews to get their views about the new framework, and to find out more about the factors that shaped their decisions.

The sample

The study was concerned with an overview of sentencing practice in the higher and lower courts respectively, and drew its sample from a lot of courts with the aim of achieving nationally representative samples. The samples from individual courts were not large enough for us to analyse differences between them, and the study was not designed to look at disparities between courts.

At the Crown Court, all offences except murder were included. In terms of the pattern of sentencing, the sample of 1,777 defendants from 18 courts, was representative of the national picture: for example, 57 per cent of the sample received immediate custody, compared with 56 per cent nationally in 1995. For community sentences the figures were 33 per cent and 30 per cent respectively (Table A3, Appendix A). The data was collected between September 1995 and January 1996.

A different approach was used in magistrates' courts. The main interest was in the more serious of the offences they deal with, where the choice of sentence is complex, rather than routine and numerous motoring offences where a fine is virtually automatic. The sample, comprising 3,000 defendants from 25 courts, is not, therefore, representative of magistrates' courts' caseloads. There is a relatively large number of cases which resulted in custody or a community penalty. So far as the analysis of offences is concerned, the main focus throughout the report is on the principal offence: in essence, where more than one offence is involved the principal offence is the one that attracts the heaviest sentence. Where several different types of offence receive the same sentence the principal offence is the one which is liable to the highest maximum penalty.

2 Recent trends in sentencing

There have been a number of major changes in the pattern of sentencing in both magistrates' courts and the Crown Court during the 1990s. The principal changes are:

- Use of immediate custody dropped slightly when the 1991 Act first came into force, but started to rise from the end of 1992 and there has been a continuing rise since then.

- Use of the suspended sentence dropped sharply when the 1991 Act came into force, and has remained at a low level.

- Average sentence lengths have risen at both higher and lower courts.

- Use of community sentences rose when the 1991 Act came into effect, and levelled off from late 1993 onwards.

- Use of fines increased at magistrates' courts (though not at the Crown Court) when the 1991 Act first came into force, but has continued its long-term decline since the end of 1992.

- Conditional discharges were initially used more following the 1991 Act, but their use has fallen at both higher and lower courts throughout the 1990s.

- Use of compensation orders has fallen at both higher and lower courts throughout the 1990s.

Figure 2.1: Trends in sentencing in magistrates' courts 1990-1996
Indictable offences only (Source: Criminal Statistics 1996)

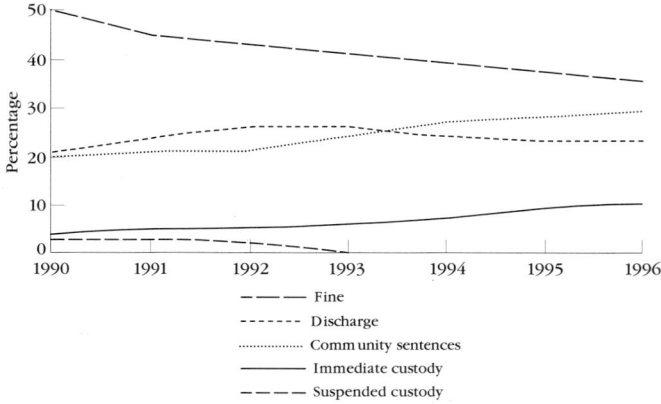

- – – Fine
- - - - Discharge
- .... Community sentences
- ———— Immediate custody
- – – – Suspended custody

Figure 2.2: Trends in sentencing in Crown Courts 1990-1996
Indictable offences only (Source: Criminal Statistics 1996)

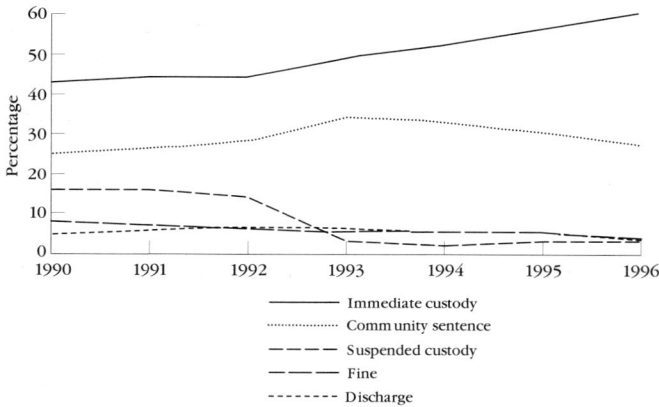

- ———— Immediate custody
- .... Community sentence
- – – – Suspended custody
- – – – Fine
- - - - Discharge

Custody

It can be seen from Figures 2.1 and 2.2 that the *initial* fall in the use of suspended custody coincided with a fall in the use of immediate custody as well. This occurred when the Criminal Justice Act 1991 was first implemented, and no doubt reflects the tough new custody threshold which applied to both immediate and suspended custody. The use of community sentences rose very sharply, and there was also a slight rise in the use of fines and discharges.

This initial fall in custody which occurred when the 1991 Act came into force was followed by a reversal in terms of immediate custody from the beginning of 1993, which continued for about nine months before levelling off and then climbing very slowly. Both suspended sentences and community sentences fell during the period when immediate custody was rising most rapidly.

Community sentences

At magistrates' courts, use of community sentences rose from 21 per cent in 1991 to 29 per cent in 1996. At the Crown Court there was a rise from 26 per cent to 34 per cent in 1993, followed by a fall to 27 per cent in 1996. This pattern is very different to that of the magistrate court.

The introduction of the combination order has contributed both to the increase in community sentences and to changes in the use of community service and probation. Figures 2.3 and 2.4 show how the relative use of probation, community service and combination orders have changed over the period, and it should be borne in mind that combination orders only became available in October 1992. Community sentences continued to increase overall at magistrates' courts between 1990 and 1996. The number of CSOs fell slightly in 1995 and 1996 but this was more than offset by an increase in the number of combination orders. Use of community sentences at the Crown Court fell steadily from a peak in 1993 over the same period. The only community sentence to increase at the Crown Court was the combination order. There is little doubt that the fall in the use of community services was linked to the significant shift to the use of immediate custody in the mid 1990s.

Figure 2.3: Relative use of community sentences at magistrates courts', 1990-1996 (indictable offences only) (Source: Criminal Statistics 1996)

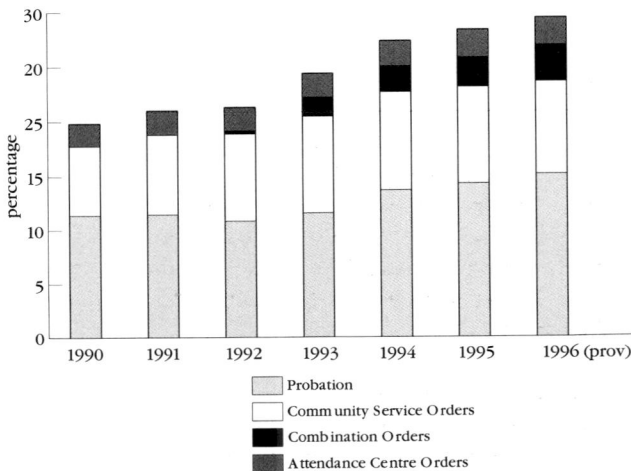

15

Figure 2.4: Relative use of community sentences at the Crown Court, 1990-1996 (indictable offences only) (Source: Criminal Statistics 1996)

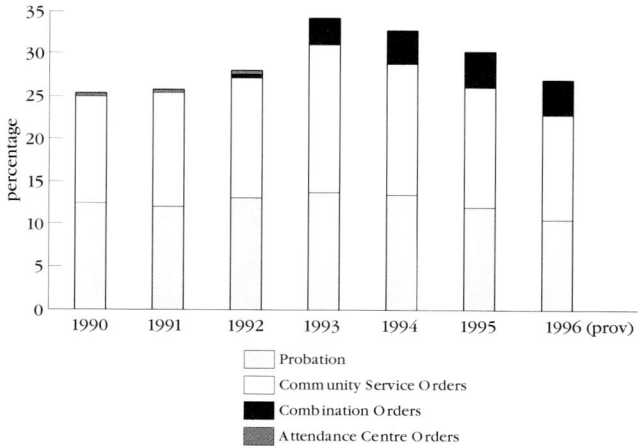

The use of attendance centre orders declined steadily between 1981 and 1991, but has remained at much the same level since the CJA, 1991 at around 2.2 per cent to 2.4 per cent.

Financial penalties

Fines

Figures 2.1 and 2.2 also show a fall in the use of fines for indictable offences. In fact, this continues a trend that was under way in the mid 1970s at both magistrates' courts and the Crown Court. For example, at magistrates' courts the use of fines for those aged 21 and over has fallen from 63 per cent in 1975 to 55 per cent of offenders in 1985 and 36 per cent in 1996. At the Crown Court the figures are 17 per cent, nine per cent and five per cent respectively.

Compensation

The use of compensation orders has also fallen in recent years, despite the fact that legislation over the years has encouraged their use, and the Criminal Justice Act 1988 strengthened the presumption in favour of awarding compensation in cases of injury, loss or damage. (Reasons must now be given where compensation is not given in qualifying cases.) The use of compensation orders fell at the Crown Court from 20 per cent to 12 per cent for violent offences and 13 per cent to eight per cent for property offences between 1990 and 1996. At magistrates' courts, use of compensation fell from 55 per cent to 51 per cent for violent offences and from 30 per cent to 22 per cent for property offences over the same period.

Discharges

The use of discharges has fallen in recent years and the trend is continuing. At magistrates' courts discharges reached a peak of 26 per cent in 1991 and 1992, and have since fallen back to 23 per cent. At the Crown Court they fell from six per cent to four per cent over this period.

Part 2

The magistrates' courts

Claire Flood-Page and Alan Mackie

3 Assessing the seriousness of a case: The decision to imprison

Although the Magistrates' Association's guidelines deal with many aggravating and mitigating factors in assessing seriousness, the seriousness with which a case is viewed is partly a subjective judgement which may differ between sentencers and may vary over time.[1] This chapter examines the factors most strongly associated with use of custody.

Figure 3.1 shows the factors which were associated with the use of custody[2]. Among the offence-related factors, custody was more likely where the

Figure 3.1: Factors associated with immediate custody
All offence types. (Source: Magistrates' courts' survey)

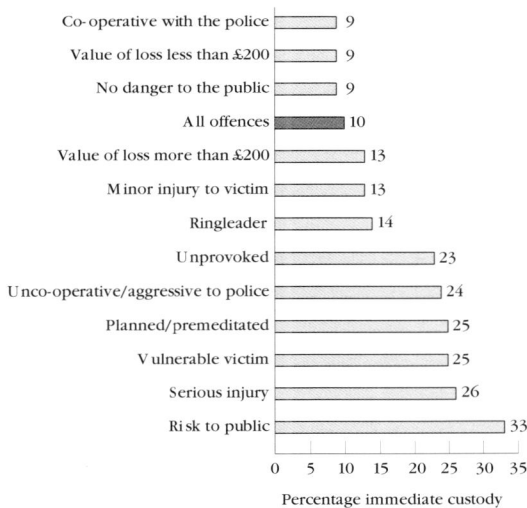

Co-operative with the police 9
Value of loss less than £200 9
No danger to the public 9
All offences 10
Value of loss more than £200 13
Minor injury to victim 13
Ringleader 14
Unprovoked 23
Unco-operative/aggressive to police 24
Planned/premeditated 25
Vulnerable victim 25
Serious injury 26
Risk to public 33

0   5   10   15   20   25   30   35
Percentage immediate custody

incident was unprovoked or pre-meditated, if the victim received a serious

---

1   A simple example of this is the concern about offending on bail which was expressed, particularly by the police, in the early 1990s. *Criminal Statistics* shows that there was an increase in the proportion of cases which received a custodial sentence in this period, partly because people sentenced for offences committed while they were on bail were dealt with more severely by the courts. In the 1994 Criminal Justice and Public Order Act, the fact that an offence was committed while the offender was on bail was formalised into an aggravating factor to be considered at sentence.

2   The factors included in these tables were initially identified by bivariate analysis to be significantly associated with the use of custody. Many of the factors which were initially identified were closely correlated. Multivariate analysis (logisitic regression) was used to identify the factors which had an independent effect on the probability of custody. These are shown in the following tables and figures.

injury or the case involved a substantial amount of loss. Turning to the offender, the fact that they were seen as posing a threat to the public was mentioned in one-third of cases which received a custodial sentence. The offender's behaviour on arrest – whether they were aggressive or refused to co-operate with the police – was also associated with a higher likelihood of custody. Those who played a minor role in the offence were less likely to receive a custodial sentence than ringleaders.

Some mitigating and aggravating factors are specific to certain offence categories. The remainder of this chapter looks at these in more detail.

Violence against the person [3]

The range of seriousness in cases of violence tends to be less than for other offences because the nature and extent of any injury will largely dictate the charge. In the sample, 40 per cent of the violence charges were assault occasioning actual bodily harm or GBHS 20, 44 per cent were common assault, 11 per cent were assault on a police officer and five per cent were grievous bodily harm (GBH). The Magistrates' Association's guidelines at the time of the study suggest that the entry point for assault on a police officer was custody but for actual bodily harm (ABH) they recommended an entry point of a community penalty. In practice, the proportion of cases of assault on a police officer resulting in custodial sentences was similar to those for GBH and ABH [4].

Figure 3.2: Violence–Factors associated with immediate custody (Source: Magistrates' courts' survey)

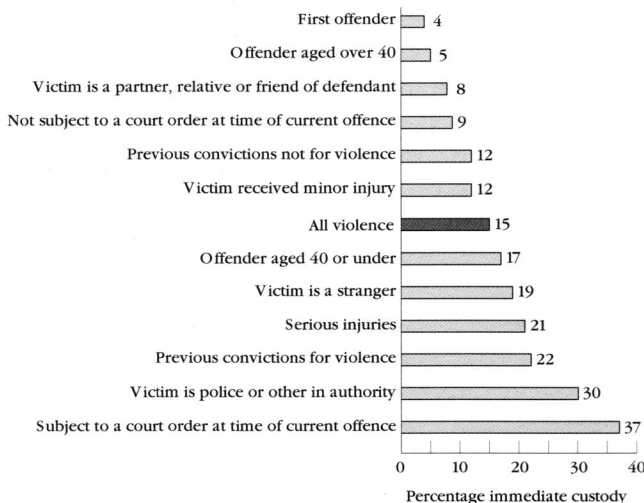

Factor	Percentage immediate custody
First offender	4
Offender aged over 40	5
Victim is a partner, relative or friend of defendant	8
Not subject to a court order at time of current offence	9
Previous convictions not for violence	12
Victim received minor injury	12
All violence	15
Offender aged 40 or under	17
Victim is a stranger	19
Serious injuries	21
Previous convictions for violence	22
Victim is police or other in authority	30
Subject to a court order at time of current offence	37

3 All of the factors which were significantly associated with the probability of a custodial sentence are shown in Table B4, Appendix B.

4 21% of cases of assaults on police officers resulted in a custodial sentence compared with 22% of GBH s20 and 17% of ABH. 10% of common assaults received a custodial sentence.

Cases where the victim sustained a more serious injury were more likely to receive a custodial penalty: in total only 12 per cent of cases where the victim received bruises, cuts or swelling received a custodial sentence compared to 21 per cent of cases where a more serious injury was involved (Figure 3.2). Over a third of those subject to a court order at the time of the current offence were given custody as were over a fifth of those with a previous conviction for violence. Assaults committed on strangers were very much more likely to result in a custodial sentence than 'domestic incidents' where the victim was the partner or a relative of the offender.

Burglary

The Magistrates' Association's guidelines give an entry point of custody for burglary of a dwelling but one of a community sentence for non-domestic burglary, and in this study burglary of a dwelling was much more likely to result in a custodial sentence.

Figure 3.3: Burglary–Factors associated with immediate custody (Source: Magistrates' courts' survey)

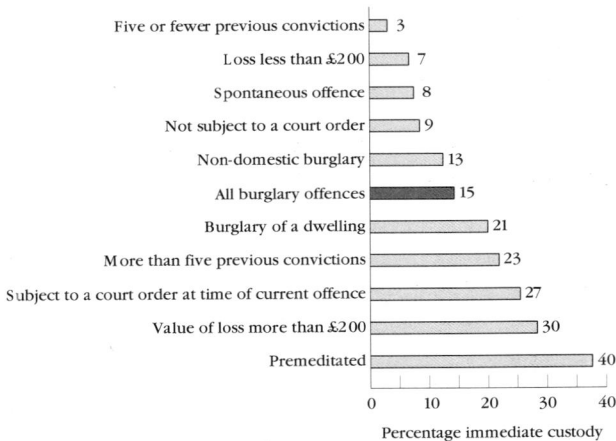

Factors mentioned in the Magistrates' Association's guidelines as indicators of a more serious offence were that the offence was:

- committed at night

- committed by a group of offenders

- executed in a professional manner

- involving ransacking or soiling the property

- where the occupants were deliberately frightened.

In this sample custody was more likely where the offender was subject to a court order when the current offence was committed. In one example, the 27-year-old offender was sentenced to 12 months imprisonment for two offences of non-domestic burglary and one of assault on a police officer. The magistrates said that the fact the offences were committed while on bail, and also while subject to a probation order, made the offences so serious that a custodial sentence was necessary. One offence involved breaking into a college store room and stealing a television; the second involved a burglary at a cafe used by disabled people. The third offence occurred when he hit the arresting police officer.

There were only five cases where premeditation was mentioned and two resulted in custody. In one example, a 19-year-old man was convicted of a burglary which involved breaking into a neighbour's house and stealing property, which was not recovered, worth £420. He had allegedly watched his neighbour's house to see when she went out. Four months previously he had received a custodial sentence for another burglary. He received four months for this latest offence.

Offenders in a quarter of cases involving loss or damage valued at more than £200 received a custodial sentence compared to just seven per cent of offenders where the loss was less than £200.

Sentencing of repeat burglars

The Crime (Sentences) Act 1997 provides for a mandatory minimum three-year custodial sentence where an offender is convicted of a third offence of burglary of a dwelling unless there are exceptional circumstances.[5] Our data indicated whether the offender had any previous burglary convictions, but not how many. There were 29 repeat burglars in this study, six of whom received a custodial sentence (21%). The majority (66%) were dealt with by some form of community penalty and four (14%) were fined. We paid particular attention to cases where magistrates did not sentence repeat burglars to custody. These will have been among the less serious burglary cases dealt with, because previous convictions for burglary would have been taken into account when mode of trial was determined and the more serious cases would have been committed to the Crown Court.

---

5   The Home Secretary announced on 30th July 1997 that the implementation of these provisions would be considered in the light of resources and the Prison Service's capacity.

Five of the 10 repeat burglars given a probation order had drug, alcohol or mental health problems. In one case a 25-year-old man with schizophrenia broke into a house and stole goods, which were later recovered, to the value of £139. The magistrates imposed a 12-month probation order to ensure that he received psychiatric treatment and to help him settle into the community. The importance of the needs of the offender when imposing such an order is underlined by the fact that, in two other cases, the defendants had drug problems and, despite having been in breach of a pre-existing probation order, were made subject of further probation orders to allow them to continue with treatment.

Where repeat burglars were fined, small amounts of property were involved, and had been recovered. None of them had any of the aggravating features mentioned in the Magistrates' Association guidelines. One of the cases, for example, involved breaking into an outhouse and stealing tools worth £110, which were quickly recovered and restored to the owner. The offender was fined £150. The magistrates described this as a 'hefty' fine on an unemployed 21-year-old man. In a second case, the offender pleaded guilty to breaking into a house along with a co-defendant. Magistrates imposed a fine of £150 because they considered the offender had been influenced by his co-defendant and was therefore less culpable.

Theft

Mode of trial guidelines issued by the Lord Chancellor's Department suggest that theft cases should normally be heard by magistrates unless any of the following conditions are met:

- the alleged theft involves a breach of trust, because the offender was in a position of authority or responsibility

- the offence was committed in a sophisticated or professional manner

- the victim was particularly vulnerable to theft or the unrecovered property was worth over £5,000.

Two-thirds of thefts in the present study involved sums of less than £100. Thefts vary so much that only very broad guidance can be given. However, an Appeal Court ruling suggests that petty theft should not normally attract a prison sentence (Wasik, 1993:323); (Upton (1980) 2cr appris 132), and the Magistrates' Association's guidelines suggest a fine as the entry point.

Figure 3.4 shows that those convicted of theft of, or from, a vehicle were most likely to receive a custodial sentence (21%). Fourteen per cent of offenders convicted of theft from a person and 10 per cent convicted of shoplifting received a custodial sentence. The average amount involved in a theft that resulted in a custodial sentence was £407 compared to £294 for other cases.

Figure 3.4: Theft-Factors associated with immediate custody (Source: Magistrates' courts' survey)

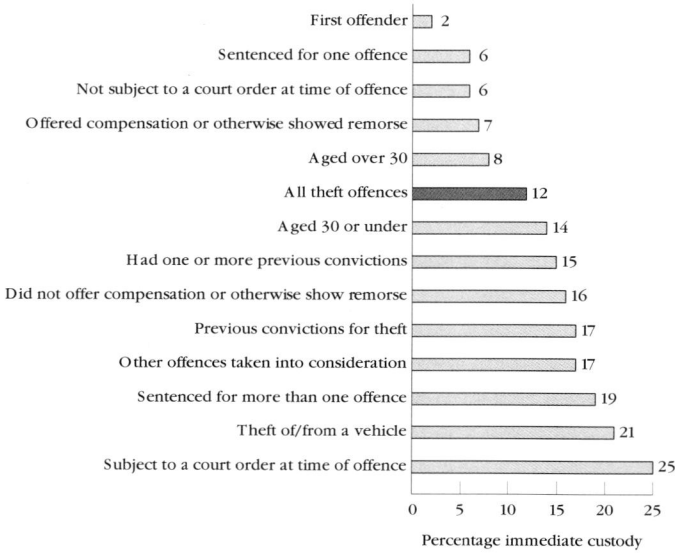

Offenders who had previous convictions were seven times as likely as first offenders to receive a custodial sentence. Where the previous convictions included theft they were almost twice as likely to receive imprisonment as offenders whose previous offences were not theft. Being subject to a court order at the time of this offence was strongly associated with the use of custody. Offenders who were sentenced for more than one offence or who had other offences taken into consideration were also more likely to receive a custodial sentence.

A third of those convicted of theft expressed remorse, and of these only seven per cent received a custodial sentence, compared to 16 per cent of those who had neither expressed remorse nor offered compensation.

Only six per cent of women convicted of theft received a prison sentence compared to 14 per cent of men. However, Table 3.1 shows that, when previous criminal records were taken into account, men and women with fewer than six previous convictions were equally likely to receive a custodial sentence. Men with six or more previous convictions were significantly more likely to receive a custodial sentence than women with similar criminal records.

Table 3.1 Proportion of men and women who received a custodial sentence for an offence of theft (Source: Magistrates' Court's survey)

No. previous convictions	Males: total no.	% custody	Females total no.	% custody
0	64	2	39	3
1	33	3	14	0
2–5	92	12	31	13
6+	231	20	43	7
Total	420	14	127	6

Theft involving a breach of trust [6]

Breach of trust was only mentioned in 12 cases (3% of the total) and only two of these resulted in a custodial penalty. Prior to the CJA 1991 a relatively high proportion of offenders (14%) convicted of theft in breach of trust were dealt with by a suspended sentence. However, in line with the sharp fall in the use of the suspended sentence, none of the offenders in the sample received one. The two cases that resulted in unsuspended custody both involved the theft of relatively large amounts of money taken from employers over a period of time. In the first case, a woman pleaded guilty to eight charges of theft from her employer and had a further 33 offences taken into consideration with a total value of £3,417, none of which was recovered. She said that she had been coerced into taking part in the offence by two other members of staff and had only received a small share of the money. This was her first offence and she was sentenced to 30 days' imprisonment. In the second case, a man received a six-week custodial sentence for the theft of £1,900 from his employer. It was his first offence and he said that he had taken the money after getting into financial difficulties. Magistrates opted for custody stating the large amount of money involved and the fact that he had taken money on a number of different occasions as their reasons for imposing a custodial sentence.

Nine of the 12 people convicted of theft involving breach of trust received community penalties [7]. Some of these had personal or financial problems. A typical example was a woman who pleaded guilty to two charges of theft from her employer totalling £350. She was charged after her employer had

---

6   The Mode of Trial guidelines suggest that the fact that a case involves a breach of trust means that it should normally be committed to the Crown Court. Therefore relatively few of these cases are dealt with by magistrates.

7   The remaining case, which resulted in a conditional discharge, was very much less serious than the cases above. A 20-year-old man had stolen £5 from his mother's purse to buy drugs. He had one previous conviction for theft committed 18 months previously. He received a 12-month conditional discharge and was ordered to pay £5 compensation.

got a private detective agency to install a hidden camera in the office, and she had lost her job as a result of the offence. Most of the money had been recovered. She was given a 12-month probation order and was ordered to pay compensation of £100. A second example was a man with two previous convictions who pleaded guilty to two charges of theft totalling £600. Several other offences were taken into consideration. He had lost his job as a result of the incident, was addicted to gambling and had large debts. He received a combination order consisting of a 12-month probation order and 60 hours community service. He was also ordered to pay £55 compensation.

Shoplifting

The Appeal Court has stated that shoplifting should only attract a custodial sentence where careful planning or execution suggest a 'professional' crime, or where the offender has a record of similar offences. Sixty-nine per cent of those people convicted of shoplifting received a fine or conditional discharge. Most shoplifting cases (80 per cent) involved the theft of goods worth less than £150. Only seven per cent of these offenders received a custodial sentence compared to 22 per cent of offenders where the loss was greater than £150.

Only two of the 22 shoplifting cases which attracted a custodial sentence showed signs of being 'professional' or planned. In the first case a male offender was sentenced to four months custody for the theft of two rings worth £2,390 from a jewellery shop. He asked to see the rings and then ran off with them. He was eventually apprehended by security guards after a struggle. He had four previous convictions and had come out of prison only one month earlier. The magistrates said that the fact that the offence was carried out in a sophisticated manner and that he had committed it while on prison licence, meant that a custodial sentence was necessary. In the second case, a woman pleaded guilty to shoplifting involving the theft of cigarettes worth £400 from a cash and carry store. She had planned the offence with a friend who was waiting outside with a car. All the property was recovered. In sentencing her to three months custody, magistrates said that the fact that it was premeditated, combined with her history of 24 previous convictions and previous failure to respond to supervision, made custody inevitable.

All those people imprisoned for shoplifting had previous convictions, and three-quarters had more than five previous convictions; 80 per cent had at least one previous conviction for shoplifting and 77 per cent were subject to a court order at the time of the current offence. In one example, the offender was sentenced for seven shoplifting offences over a nine-month period and one offence of failing to appear at court from bail. The value involved was £530, all of which had been recovered. She had a long-term drug problem, for which she received methadone treatment and was under stress at the time of the offence because she was living with her husband who had schizophrenia. She had five previous convictions which included shoplifting, the most recent being 15 months earlier when she had received a community service order. On imposing a six-month custodial sentence, magistrates said the offences were serious and her criminal record showed that she would not respond to a community sentence.

All five offenders who were imprisoned for a single offence of shoplifting had previous convictions for shoplifting. In one example, which was described as a 'straightforward case of shoplifting', the male offender pleaded guilty to theft of goods worth £28 from a shop. The solicitor said that he had been experiencing serious financial difficulties and was addicted to drugs. All the property was recovered. In sentencing him to four months' custody, magistrates cited his history of 19 previous convictions which included a recent custodial sentence for shoplifting.

Fraud or deception

Only nine per cent of those convicted of fraud or deception received a custodial sentence. Three of these involved fraud or forgery. In the first example, a 29-year-old man pleaded guilty to three charges of fraud in which he had defrauded the Department of Social Security of £13,000. He had three previous convictions for motoring offences. The magistrates said that the sum involved and the fact that the fraud had continued over a long period, made custody inevitable. In the other two cases, co-defendants pleaded guilty to two offences of forgery. After they had been made redundant, they had written letters to the competitors of their ex-employer with information which would help them to undercut the company. They had also made false statements that the firm was about to cease trading. In total, 29 letters bearing the forged signature of the company director were written. The company estimated this had cost them at least £5,000 in lost business. Magistrates said that the offence was deliberate and systematic. They each received four months.

The other four cases which resulted in a prison sentence involved receiving or handling stolen goods. All the offenders sentenced to custody were convicted of more than one offence compared to 52 per cent of those who received a non-custodial sentence. Five out of seven offenders sentenced to custody were subject to a court order at the time that they committed the current offence compared to 14 per cent of those who received some sentence.

Drugs

Only two per cent of drug offenders in the sample received a custodial sentence (the same as the national figure for 1995). The Appeal Court has made it clear that most offences relating to Class A drugs, such as heroin, are not suitable to be dealt with in magistrates' courts unless the offence involves the possession of a small amount of drugs for the offender's personal use[8]. The Magistrates' Association's guidelines suggest a community penalty as the starting point for sentence in such cases. Only five per cent of the drugs cases in this sample involved supplying drugs to others. Most were related to possession of class B drugs, such as cannabis and amphetamines for which the Magistrates' Association's guidelines suggest that the starting point for sentence should be a fine, but would be influenced by the amount of drugs involved. Amarah (1982) suggests that a fine will usually be the appropriate penalty unless the offender has repeated convictions for possession of drugs.

Possession of drugs

Of the offenders sentenced for possession of drugs, 73 per cent were fined. More severe sentences were sometimes imposed on those with a criminal record which included similar offences, or those subject to a court order at the time of the current offence. Of those offenders who received a custodial or a community sentence, 27 per cent were subject to a court order at the time of the current offence whereas only six per cent of those who received a fine or discharge were subject to a court order. Only seven per cent of those receiving a custodial or community sentence were first offenders compared to 31 per cent of those who received a fine or discharge.

The two offenders who received custodial sentences for possession were either sentenced for other offences at the same time, or else were in custody when they were sentenced. One offender received a 14-day custodial sentence for possession of cannabis to run concurrently with a three-month sentence imposed for a breach of a community service order. In the second case, a man received a six-week custodial sentence for possession of drugs. He had 12 previous convictions, including some drugs offences, and was in custody for other offences when he was sentenced for the current offence.

Supplying drugs

Only one of the five offenders sentenced for supplying a class B drug received a custodial sentence. He had grown a number of cannabis plants in his home and then sold the drug. Although the defence stated that he had

---

8   Amarah (1982) 4 Cr App R.

not received money for the drugs, magistrates concluded that the case was so serious that a custodial sentence was justified because the number of plants and equipment found in the house suggested that he was cultivating the plants to sell cannabis. In a similar case at the same court, the offender pleaded guilty to one charge of supplying class B drugs and one of simple possession. The facts of the case were that a number of cannabis plants had been found growing in his bedroom. The defence said that the drugs were for his own use but he also supplied them to friends. In this instance magistrates appeared to accept that the drugs were not supplied on a commercial basis, and he was fined £240.

The suspended sentence

Earlier work on suspended sentences (Moxon, 1988) found that they were used typically for two groups of offenders; people with no previous history of offending convicted of a serious offence (in particular, theft involving a breach of trust) or those with a long criminal history but where there was evidence of a change in lifestyle which meant that their offending may be coming to an end. Moxon said that:

> *The impression gained ... was that on occasions the suspended sentence was simply seen as the least bad option: judges may have been loath to opt for a conditional discharge, which could be seen as a let-off; prospects of recovering a fine might have been slight, and if probation or community service had been tried previously, failure to complete the order might preclude further use.... The effect of using the suspended sentence in these circumstances may be to tie the hands of the sentencer on the next occasion. (Moxon, 1988:71-2)*

Suspended sentences were never widely used in magistrates' courts but following the CJA 1991 they became very rare: in 1990, 0.9 per cent of all defendants sentenced in magistrates' courts received a fully suspended sentence compared with 0.1 per cent in 1995.[9] The CJA 1991 did not give any indication of what constituted 'exceptional circumstances' and, in a Court of Appeal case shortly after the Act came into force, Lord Taylor CJ said that it was not possible to define exceptional circumstances but that, on their own, youth, good character and a guilty plea did not constitute grounds for suspending a prison sentence.[10]

In interviews, magistrates said that 'exceptional circumstances' would include 'family or business reasons', 'that the offender demonstrated a change in attitude' and 'war veteran suffering from post-traumatic stress

---

9   In the sample, a suspended sentnce was the principal sentence in only 10 (0.3%) cases.
10   Okimikan (1992) 14 Cr App R (S) 453.

syndrome'. A common example of the kind of case that might attract a suspended sentence was of a woman with young children, where imprisonment would harm the children and perhaps cause them to go into care. Such reasons may not fall within the strict Court of Appeal guidelines: in Lowery[11] a police officer with 20 years' service, who had been responsible for collecting fines, pleaded guilty to 11 counts of false accounting. An immediate custodial sentence of three months was imposed. His wife had become disabled and he had stolen the money to help pay for adaptations to their house to meet her needs. As a result of the offence he had lost his house and his job, and his pension had been frozen until he was 60. He was receiving psychiatric help after making two suicide attempts. The Court of Appeal said that this did not amount to the 'exceptional circumstances' required to suspend the sentence because offences involving a breach of trust often resulted in consequences far beyond the immediate sentence. However, the Court did reduce the sentence to allow for the offender's immediate release (reported in Wasik, 1993:161-2).

Magistrates were divided over suspended sentence. Some saw it as 'an extra strong conditional discharge' which aimed to deter offenders from committing more crime and/or to give them an opportunity to show that they had 'reformed'. Others, however, maintained that imposing a suspended sentence could make sentencing the offender for subsequent offences very difficult, either during the period of the suspension or at its conclusion. This was a particular problem where a suspended sentence had been imposed for want of a more appropriate sentence rather than because custody was really justified, a situation which some magistrates belived occured.

There were only ten examples of suspended sentences in this sample. In these cases custody had been suspended either because the offender provided care for someone else or because they were ill or receiving treatment for drug or alcohol addiction which would be interrupted by imprisonment. In one example, a 43-year-old man was convicted of assault occasioning actual bodily harm on an acquaintance who had racially abused him. The defendant wielded a knife to the victim, who received a small cut to his face. The magistrates found 'exceptional circumstances' to suspend the custodial sentence in the racial provocation of the victim, the defendant's age and the fact that he provided full-time care for his disabled wife.

In a second case, an offender was convicted of handling goods for which he received a two-month custodial sentence, suspended for 12 months. His solicitor said that he would find it difficult to comply with a community sentence as he had to look after his learning-disabled son. Magistrates said that they had taken account of the fact that the defendant's son and new born baby would suffer if he went to prison.

---

11   R v Lowery (1993) Crim LR 225.

In another case a woman pleaded guilty to two charges of assault occasioning actual bodily harm on a neighbour and the arresting police officer and one charge of shoplifting. The offence was aggravated by her being in breach of a conditional discharge and a deferred sentence. The defendant had alcohol and drug problems and had attempted suicide while in police custody. She had a young daughter who was the subject of care proceedings. In this case the magistrates said that the offences were so serious that only custody was suitable. However they said that, because she needed to receive continuous treatment for her alcohol and drug problems, the sentence would be suspended. In another case, the offender had been depressed and drinking heavily following an operation for stomach cancer. He was convicted of failing to provide a specimen and driving while disqualified. Magistrates considered that his illness and stress on the family constituted exceptional circumstances.

The suspended sentence and other sentences

A suspended sentence may be passed in combination with another sentence such as a fine and/or a compensation order, and it can be imposed in road traffic cases together with disqualification. Of the ten offenders who received a suspended sentence, four were also ordered to pay compensation, two were fined and one received a probation order. Only two received a suspended sentence on its own.

Length of custodial sentences

The average length of a custodial sentence has risen slightly in recent years: in 1995 the average sentence for a man over 21 was 2.8 months compared to 2.6 months in 1990. For women there was an increase from 2.3 to 2.4 months over this period.

The Magistrates' Association's guidelines on sentence length assume a plea of not guilty and state that the sentence should be reduced by up to a third if a guilty plea was entered at an early stage. One of the 12 courts had altered their guidelines so that the entry points assumed a guilty plea and stated that the recommended sentence should be increased if either the plea was entered at a late stage or a trial had been held. The Justices' Clerk in this court said that, because the majority of defendants plead guilty, the guidelines had been altered to promote consistency in applying the discount. One magistrate in this area commented:

> The Clerk maintains that 97 per cent of cases that come here are guilty pleas anyway. Our guidelines must be correct in 97 per cent of the cases. If our guidelines were based on a not guilty plea, they'd be wrong in 97 per cent of the cases.

In this study there were only 30 contested cases resulting in a custodial sentence – not enough to measure the impact of plea on sentence length: the average sentence length where the offender pleaded guilty was 3.7 months compared with 3.8 months where they pleaded not guilty. There was also no difference in the proportion receiving custody. With automatic early release the discount could only very exceptionally reduce the time spent in prison by more than one month. (An offender sentenced to four months, as against the maximum of six months, serves two months in prison compared to a maximum of three months if they plead not guilty and receive the longest sentence possible.)

4 Community sentences

An overview of how community sentences fit into the overall framework, and recent trends in their use, was given in Part 1. This chapter looks at the factors which were associated with the use of one type of community order in preference to another.

When were community penalties used?

The relatively low use of custody in the lower courts means that aggravating factors tend to push cases above the community sentence threshold, whereas in the Crown Court similar factors might push cases over the custody threshold. Those convicted of burglary, violence or fraud were more likely than those convicted of other offences to get a community sentence (Figure 4.1). Aggravating factors which made cases more likely to

Figure 4.1: Factors associated with use of community sentence rather than a fine or discharge (Source: Magistrates' courts' survey)

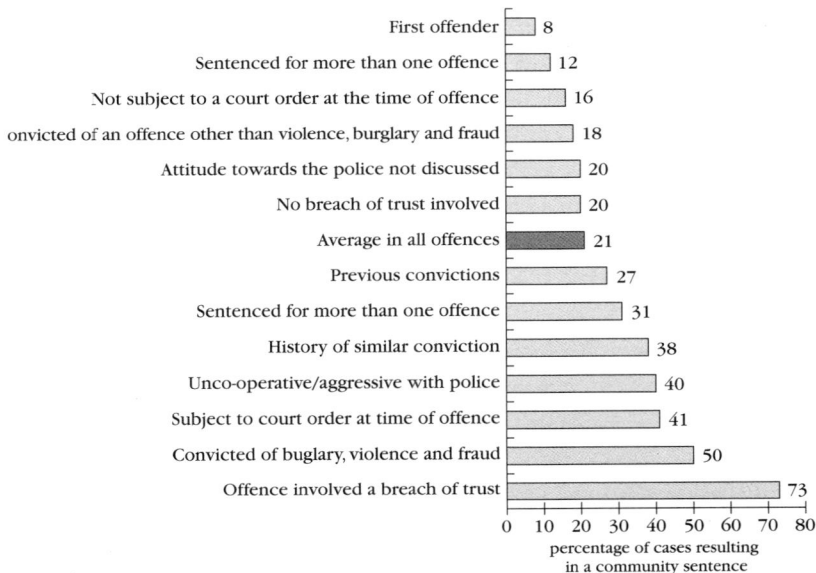

Factor	Percentage
First offender	8
Sentenced for more than one offence	12
Not subject to a court order at the time of offence	16
Convicted of an offence other than violence, burglary and fraud	18
Attitude towards the police not discussed	20
No breach of trust involved	20
Average in all offences	21
Previous convictions	27
Sentenced for more than one offence	31
History of similar conviction	38
Unco-operative/aggressive with police	40
Subject to court order at time of offence	41
Convicted of buglary, violence and fraud	50
Offence involved a breach of trust	73

percentage of cases resulting in a community sentence

result in a community sentence rather than a fine included lack of co-operation with the police, breach of trust, or having other offences taken into consideration: 27 per cent of repeat offenders received a community sentence compared to eight per cent of first offenders. A community sentence was particularly likely where there were previous convictions for similar offences.

It is important to note that the factors listed indicate *the outcome when the factor is present.* They do not relate to numbers of cases. So, for example, 73 per cent of cases in which breach of trust was mentioned resulted in a community sentence. But in many cases (e.g. burglary) breach of trust is irrelevant so would not feature in any way.

The choice between community sentences

Table 4.1 shows some characteristics of people who received different community orders. Those receiving a combination order were more likely to be sentenced for more than one offence and to have previous criminal convictions than those given a CSO. They were also more likely to have been charged with offences of violence or serious motoring offences such as driving while disqualified, whereas a greater proportion of those who received probation and CSOs had committed property offences. This is consistent with the 1992 National Standards which indicate that combination orders are a 'higher tariff' sentence, to be used where the offender is at risk of custody, as violence and motoring offences had the highest rates of custody in the sample.

Table 4.1 Characteristics of those receiving combination orders, community service orders and probation orders (Source: Magistrates' courts' survey)

	% combination order	% community service order	% probation order
Offence-related factors			
Offence Type			
Violence	14	5	10
Burglary, fraud or theft	31	40	44
Motoring	53	37	28
Sentenced for more than			
one offence	83	63	66
Offender-related factors			
Unemployed	65	65	81
Mentally ill/stressed	16	10	14
Single	10	38	52
No previous convictions	10	21	10
Long time since previous			
offence	3	4	5
Unco-operative with the police			
at arrest	10	15	9
In custody prior to sentence	14	4	12
Under 21	30	18	16

Fourteen per cent of those who received a probation order were described in court as either being mentally ill or under stress at the time of sentencing or to have been so when they committed the offence. Probation orders were also used more for the unemployed. CSOs were frequently used for first offenders who had been convicted of quite serious offences, in particular fraud or deception.[1]

Magistrates' views on community sentences

In order to provide a fuller understanding of how the different community sentence options were used, we sought the views of magistrates. In detailed analysis, it was found that while the use of combination orders could be predicted quite well; it was harder to predict who would receive a probation order or CSO. This finding that the choice between probation and community service was not always clear-cut was reinforced in interviews. (See Table B9, Appendix B)

---

1   20% of first offenders sentenced to community service were convicted of fraud or deception, 10% of violence and 7% of burglary.

Magistrates said that a CSO was primarily concerned with the punishment of the offender with an element of reparation:

Reparation should be seen very much as a function for community service but it is not always possible to do that.

I see community service more as reparation [than punishment]. It is achieving self-esteem, if they don't have any, by doing a job for other people .... I am an optimist and always hope that one or two of them will change their ways having seen people worse off than themselves.

Another stated that CS was imposed:

....where the offender needs to be taught a lesson. It is more punitive than probation. A community service order is paying something back to the community.

The belief that community service could help the offender to reform was fairly widespread; magistrates saw the opportunity to participate in community work as a source of self-esteem and as enabling the development of self-discipline. This was particularly true for unemployed offenders, where the demands of having to attend regularly for CSO sessions was seen as an opportunity to develop a more disciplined routine and to 'get into the habit of working':

....it is a taste of actually doing a job... community service helps them to establish a work ethic.

The way I look at it is that they build up their own self-esteem and at the same time they do unpaid work for others and the community can see them doing it.

Magistrates in five of the 28 interview groups told anecdotes about offenders who had learnt a skill doing community service and subsequently found employment and stopped offending. However, one group was sceptical about the value of giving work to an offender as training because it could not continue at the end of the order.

A common complaint was that the type of work that offenders undertook on community service was not sufficiently demanding. It was important that:

....the community out there see it as a punishment. When [the general public] see what work is about, they say, 'Well, I'm decorating my house this weekend. That's not punishment'.

There were wide differences between magistrates in their knowledge of the types of schemes run locally: some had visited schemes while others knew little about the work that was available. Magistrates who had visited CSO work-placements were frequently impressed. As one remarked:

There is some good work done. They have freed all of the brooks and streams that have got clogged up and made paths which nobody else would ever do.

Nevertheless, there was sometimes a suspicion that a CSO could be completed merely by attending a centre and *'drinking cups of coffee'*, or a regret that the work done under an order was not physically demanding. The National Standards for community service recognise this concern:

....each probation service should regularly consult local sentencers with a view to agreeing a wide range of preferred placements which will enhance confidence in community service. The range of placements should include at least one option with hard manual work and consideration should be given to choosing placements which will enhance public confidence in community service. (Home Office, 1995:34)

The concerns expressed by magistrates suggests that there was a continuing need for close liaison between probation services and magistrates in order to build sentencers' confidence in the value of CSOs as punishment. Two areas have set up multi-agency community sentence demonstration projects, with a view to improving liaison between the Probation Service and sentencers. The aim is to improve sentencers' and public confidence in community penalties, both by ensuring that schemes reflect their concerns and by improving liaison between the courts and the Probation Service.

Magistrates in two of the 12 areas also expressed concern about the numbers of offenders who were said to be unsuitable for CSO in pre-sentence reports. They suggested that a wider range of placements should be available so that women (especially those with child-care responsibilities) and people suffering some forms of illness or disability would not be excluded. This problem was highlighted by a report on women offenders by HMI Probation (1991) which noted sentencers' reluctance to give women offenders CSOs because (in the view of courts and probation officers) they would be given 'inappropriate' tasks.[2] A later report, commissioned by the Association of Chief Officers of Probation (Barker, 1993) found that, of the five areas studied, only one made explicit provision for women. This was a particular problem in rural areas. The current National Standards for

---

2 The National Standards for Community Sentences at that time insisted on initial group work placements for all offenders. Because of the small numbers of women doing a CSO at any one time, this meant that women were placed in groups consisting mainly of men.

Community Penalties state that CSO schemes should be reviewed regularly to ensure that there is a broad range of placements available for young offenders, people with disabilities, women, single parents and offenders from minority groups (Home Office, 1995:35). In this study, women were no less likely than men to be given a combination order or CSO.

Probation orders

There was a clear consensus that probation is an individualised disposal for offenders with problems requiring help and support:

> *It is a welfare disposal, simply that somebody is in touch to keep an eye on the person and perhaps preventing a further crime.*

Most magistrates believed that probation and CSO were appropriate for offences of similar seriousness. This is a major change as, before the CJA 1991, a CSO was an alternative to custody whereas probation was an alternative to sentencing for any offender who might benefit from it. The choice between the two sanctions depended on the needs of the offender rather than the seriousness of the offence:

> *If it's purely a punishment that is required, it will be a community service order and if it was purely help it would be a probation order.*

> *Where someone's life is fairly uncluttered or uncomplicated but they've done something wrong community service is appropriate. For someone who has got themselves into a mess, has lots of problems in their life and has committed the same crime, then you might say that this person really needs to talk this through and needs some more structure in their lives. Probation is better from that point of view.*

Some were sceptical that probation served as a punishment at all:

> *One of the dilemmas is the extent to which it is possible to have a restriction on liberty, because realistically they see them once a week, at the most... it is very hard to see that as a real restriction of liberty.*

Another magistrate expressed this view more forcibly:

> *I do think that it is a bit of a laugh when probation is talked about as a form of deprivation of liberty when you consider that they come down to the probation office perhaps about half an hour a fortnight. How on earth anyone can consider that to be a deprivation of liberty I do not know.*

This group of magistrates said that it was much easier to appreciate a CSO as a 'punishment' because it involved a definite time commitment as well as physical work.

On the other hand, some magistrates believed that many offenders found complying with even the simplest form of probation difficult because of their disorganised lifestyles:

> [Probation] *isn't weekly tea and chat. The meetings are restrictive in themselves because a lot of people have the type of lifestyle where they have never had to turn up at the same place every week. They have never had to do what they are told and have never had to keep in touch. The National Standards have tightened things up so that breach proceedings will take place where the conditions are not adhered to.*

> *There is still an attitude that says that probation is the 'soft option', its just seeing the probation officer a couple of times a month or something and nothing very much happens. The reality of what probation orders these days mean by way of commitment of time and working through their criminal behaviour, and confrontation of how they have got into their situation is not recognised by the bench as a real punishment.*

> *Probation is more challenging than serving a few months in prison where they don't have to do anything, everything is done for them.*

Ambivalence about the extent to which probation could be viewed as a punishment meant that some magistrates had very little faith in it. For example, one group of magistrates said that:

> *A vast majority of this bench believe that it is tea and chat and the practical result is that straight probation orders are given for lower tariff offences than they might be.*

From a different perspective, a recent survey of offenders on probation found that a majority of offenders appreciated the help that probation officers gave (Mair and May, 1997). The most frequently mentioned 'good point' about probation was that it gave offenders someone to talk to about problems. A third mentioned that they had received practical help with problems and about a fifth said that they had been helped to keep out of trouble and avoid reoffending. Nine out of 10 offenders thought that their current probation order was useful. The most commonly mentioned negative point was the time taken to attend the sessions and the inconvenience of travelling to attend (Mair and May, 1997:vi).

Probation as a sentence for minor offenders

Six of the 28 groups of magistrates regretted the fact that the CJA 1991 had limited the use of probation for less serious offences. There was a feeling that, prior to the CJA 1991, the probation order had been a useful option for some first offenders, in particular minor drug offenders, as they could be offered some support to divert them from offending early in their criminal career.

Additional requirements to probation

A court may require that during the whole, or part, of a probation order, the offender must comply 'with such requirements as the court, with regard to the circumstances of the case, considers desirable' (Powers of the Criminal Courts Act 1973 s3(1)). Of the probation orders in the sample, 27 per cent included additional requirements. Whether or not the court imposes additional requirements, offenders may take part in organised group activities during the course of their probation. In a recent survey, 40 per cent of offenders on probation had taken part in a special programme of activity (Mair and May, 1997). The type of additional requirement which can be made varies between probation areas depending upon what activities are provided by each service.

Men convicted of motoring offences were particularly likely to be required to attend a motor project, making it the most frequent additional requirement (Figure 4.2). A fifth of additional requirements were to receive treatment for alcohol dependency while 13 per cent related to treatment for drug dependency[3].

Figure 4.2: Type of additional requirement attached to probation orders (Source: Magistrates' courts' survey) (Total of 78 orders)

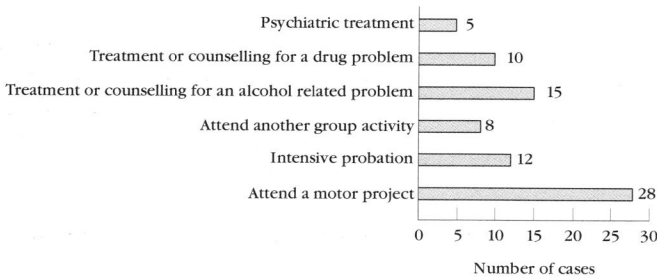

---

3   'Dependency' was broadly construed in the provisions of the Act and includes cases where the offender 'has a propensity towards the misuse of drugs or alcohol'.

Additional requirements were essentially used to tailor the order to address specific aspects of the offender's behaviour. For example, one magistrate said the purpose of additional requirements was:

> ....*to mould behaviour and change the offender for the future. They are needs based and not a punitive thing.*

In only one court did the magistrates say they imposed additional requirements *solely* to make the order more onerous. More commonly magistrates said that, while additional requirements were primarily about needs, their incidental effect was to make the order more punitive. As one magistrate said:

> *We are keen to say to an offender, 'We want to help you, but there must be an element of punishment within the order'.*

Courts differed in their use of additional requirements: while three of the 25 courts did not use them at all in the cases surveyed, six made additional requirements to more than 40 per cent of their probation orders. HMI Probation (1995) found differing policies between probation services. Some probation officers resisted the use of additional requirements and rarely recommended them in pre-sentence reports. Only seven out of the 10 services in that study had issued guidance on when to use additional requirements. Some probation services, experiencing difficulty in shaking off the idea that probation with additional requirements should be an 'alternative to custody' (as suggested by the CJA 1982), were proposing additional requirements for offences which were 'so serious' that a custodial sentence was more appropriate (HMI Probation, 1995:30, 32).

Combination orders

Magistrates liked the new order because it enabled them to reconcile the differing aims of CS and probation:

> *In the past it has been quite difficult to choose between probation and community service. One felt that it was serious enough to require community service, but that the person involved really needed probation intervention to tackle some of the reasons for the offending.*

The majority of magistrates did not see the aims of helping and punishment as mutually exclusive:

I don't see why someone can't be given an irksome regime and still be helped. As magistrates it is our duty to punish and rehabilitate, so in that sense it is an ideal sentence.

Whereas earlier research found that probation officers saw combination orders as a very demanding sentence (Mair, Sibbitt and Crisp, 1995,: unpublished), magistrates in this study were divided about whether combination orders occupied a higher place on the tariff than other community sentences. For example, one group of magistrates reported that:

We would not use [a combination order] *because it was stiffer, but because it focuses the attention on the need to pay something back to society, and the other part of it was where they needed help ... It provides a means of helping the individual.*

Others did feel the combination order as a more severe disposal which should be reserved for serious offenders:

It is a more intensive form of sentencing, so it should be reserved for serious offences that tend to be dealt with in the Crown Court.

It should only be kept for the very top ones. There is a lot of input, a lot of man hours go into combination orders and I think that you have to be careful not to waste it.

Most probation officers thought that making additional requirements could become the straw that broke the camel's back, causing offenders to give up trying to complete combination orders because they were too onerous (Mair, Sibbitt and Crisp, 1995: unpublished). However, in the present study, magistrates imposed additional requirements with 14 per cent of combination orders: four of these were to attend a motor project, one for an alcohol education group, one for an intensive probation and two for another type of group activity.

Attendance centre orders

Criminal Statistics show that, in 1995, 0.6 per cent of 18 - 20-year-olds sentenced for all offences in magistrates' courts received an attendance centre order. There are only 26 senior attendance centres in England and Wales so the order is not available as an option to all courts. The order should not be made if the offender has to travel for more than 90 minutes to reach a centre (Attendance Centre Circular 5/95). Magistrates said that they would also be unlikely to use the order if it would be expensive to travel to the centre. While they are at the centre offenders have to participate in various activities. As one magistrate explained:

> *With the attendance centre they do have to give up a couple of hours and travelling time and it interferes with their normal activities. There is a minimum standard of behaviour towards staff. It wouldn't exactly suit me if I were running a school, but there are minimum standards of dress. Rules are imposed and, if they are not adhered to, action is taken. Ultimately the order could be revoked and the offender brought back to court. The offenders are occupied for the time. How gainfully occupied they are is a matter for assessment. The attendance centre order is not a non-starter, but it could be a lot more credible.*

These magistrates expressed concerns about the type of activities. For example, in one area the magistrates regretted the fact that the offenders did not do manual work:

> *Years ago, at the police college where its run, they used to clean out the stables, clean out the kennels. There are now grooms employed so the tasks like doing a bit of whitewashing are not there any more. When we went there, what we saw was a bit of woodwork, a game of football and a discussion group.*

As a community penalty, the court has to be sure that the offence meets the general requirements of seriousness that apply to all community sentences. Most attendance centre orders are made in the youth court and so there were only three attendance centre orders in the sample. One involved a 20-year-old offender who pleaded guilty to two charges of theft and one charge of criminal damage committed while he was on bail for another offence. He had four previous convictions including one for theft. Although this initially seemed to be a serious case, the thefts were fairly minor: he had stolen goods worth £24 from a shop and, in making his escape from the premises, he had damaged a door which cost £100 to repair. Magistrates imposed an attendance centre order of 36 hours and ordered the offender to pay £100 compensation.

In the second case, a 19-year-old offender pleaded guilty to driving while disqualified, providing false details to the police, driving without insurance and breach of a conditional discharge. He had three previous convictions including a recent conviction for aggravated vehicle taking, for which he had been disqualified from driving. He was employed and earning £56 per week, and his solicitor had explained on his behalf that he was 'very successful' at work. His solicitor requested an attendance centre order to keep him away from hardened criminals. Several magistrates reflected this view. They said that attendance centres were sometimes preferable for young offenders because, if they did a CSO, they would have mixed with more experienced, older offenders.

Magistrates imposed a 36 hour attendance centre order on a 20-year-old for driving while disqualified and giving false details charges as well as a fine of £180 for the offence of driving without insurance. He was also disqualified from driving for a further six months.

5 Fines and discharges

Four-fifths of cases in magistrates' courts result in a fine (Figure 5.1). For many of the offences magistrates deal with, especially summary motoring, fines are almost invariably used. Although violent, sexual and property offences attract a much wider range of sentences the fine has fallen in recent years. The use of the conditional discharge increased steadily until 1993, since when there has been a slight fall. Despite the relative importance of the fine and discharges they have attracted little attention from research and there is little appellate guidance. In order to be able to impose a discharge, the court must find that, having considered the nature of the offence and the character of the offender, it would be *'inexpedient to inflict punishment'* (PCCA 1973 s 1A).

Figure 5.1: Proportionate use of fine or discharge at magistrates courts by offence type
(Source: Criminal Statistics 1996)

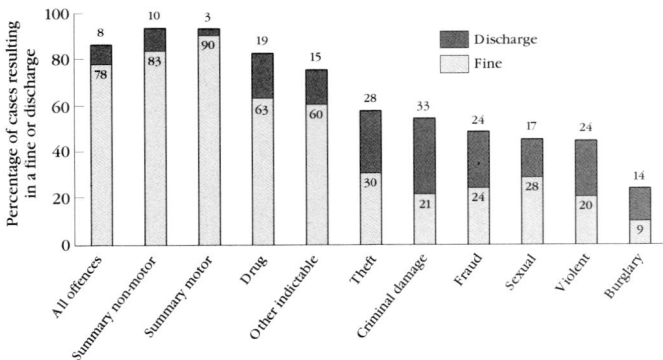

Fines

Figure 5.2 shows the factors that were associated with the use of fines. These tended to be the obverse of the factors associated with custody: fines were given to first offenders and those convicted of less serious (mostly summary) offences – low-level motoring, possession of drugs or summary (non-motoring) offences. Factors which have previously been seen to aggravate an offence, for example, being unco-operative or aggressive to the police on arrest, being subject to a court order at the time of the offence, posing a danger to the public or having other offences taken into consideration at sentencing – made a fine less likely. Those with personal problems (e.g. mental illness or significant family responsibilities) were also less likely to be fined.

Figure 5.2: Factors associated with use of fines rather than another sentence (Source: Magistrates' courts survey)

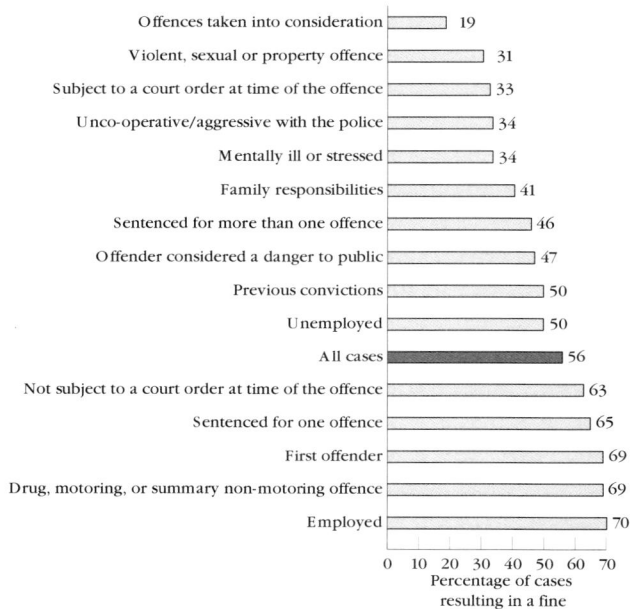

	Percentage of cases resulting in a fine
Offences taken into consideration	19
Violent, sexual or property offence	31
Subject to a court order at time of the offence	33
Unco-operative/aggressive with the police	34
Mentally ill or stressed	34
Family responsibilities	41
Sentenced for more than one offence	46
Offender considered a danger to public	47
Previous convictions	50
Unemployed	50
All cases	56
Not subject to a court order at time of the offence	63
Sentenced for one offence	65
First offender	69
Drug, motoring, or summary non-motoring offence	69
Employed	70

Fining people who are unemployed

Following the CJA 1991, the use of fines for unemployed offenders rose sharply from 30 per cent to 43 per cent of *indictable* offences sentenced at magistrates' courts. After the implementation of the CJA 1993 which abolished unit fines, the proportion of unemployed offenders fined fell to 32 per cent (*Statistical Bulletin* 20/1994). The same study also found that employed offenders were more likely to be fined. Figures 5.3 and 5.4 show that unemployed offenders were three times as likely to receive a conditional discharge whether or not they had previous convictions. Unemployed first offenders were more likely to receive a community sentence than were first offenders with a job. Magistrates in seven of the 12 areas said that sometimes they would use conditional discharges where they felt that the offender could not afford to pay a fine. In four of these areas, magistrates regarded this as bad sentencing practice but said that they sometimes felt it was the only practical option:

> *We are more often than not forced rather than led on the decision to fine or discharge by the means of the defendant. You can't get blood out of stone so, even if a fine was the most appropriate sentence, we have to resort to a conditional discharge.*

The Crime (Sentences) Act 1997 contains proposals for a range of new sentences for persistent petty offenders which will go some way to solving this sentencing problem. Where the court would consider a fine to be the most suitable sentence but the offender has existing fines which have not been paid and could not pay a further fine, the options of disqualification from driving, a curfew order and a maximum of 100 hours' community service will be available.

Figure 5.3: Sentencing of first offenders by employment status (Source: Magistrates' courts survey)

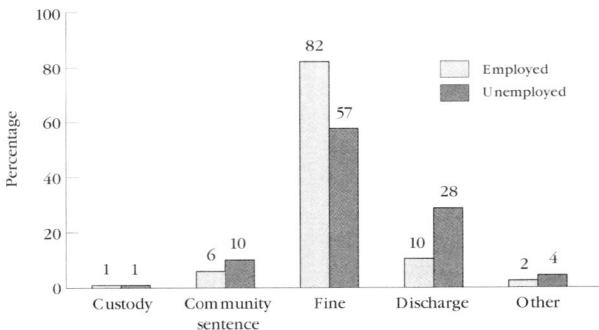

Figure 5.4: Sentencing of repeat offenders by employment status (Source: Magistrates' courts survey)

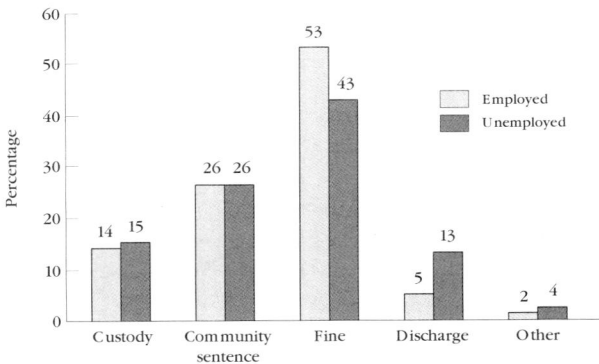

Fixing the amount

Following the abolition of unit fines in 1993, courts have more discretion in how they set fines in relation to means. The Magistrates' Association issued revised guidelines for fines in 1993 which courts were able to vary to reflect local economic conditions. The most recent guidelines (April 1997) provide for a more structured approach to relating fines to means. Fines are set according to three income bands:

- low income – about £100 per week

- average income – about £250 per week

- high income – about £600 per week

These figures have not been discounted for a guilty plea, and refer to net income. Charman et al. (1996:2) examined the guidance available to magistrates in courts throughout England and Wales and found that, while 55 per cent of courts had adopted the Magistrates' Association guidelines wholesale for setting the level of fines, 28 per cent had made significant modifications to them.[1] An informal unit fines approach was retained by 17 per cent.

Four of the 12 courts where interviews were undertaken in the present study had broadly adopted the fines recommended in the Magistrates' Association's 1993 guidelines, though three of these had adjusted the recommended fines to reflect local average income. The fourth felt that it was important to promote consistency over the country by sticking to the guidelines wherever possible.

Four courts had gone further than simply adjusting the levels of fines to reflect local average income, and had altered indicators of seriousness or 'entry levels' for different offences to take account of local factors. For example, in one court the entry point for drugs offences was 'tougher' than neighbouring jurisdictions; in another, the entry point for common assault was increased from a fine to a community penalty.

Four of the 12 courts had retained some type of informal unit fines system. One of these had continued to use a strict unit fines system so that, where the magistrates felt that a fine was appropriate, the local guidelines provided an 'entry point' in units. Sentencers then calculated the defendant's disposable weekly income within a range of £4 to a maximum of £100 as provided in the 1991 legislation. The other three courts had a less rigid formula for relating fines to weekly income. In one, guidelines suggested a range of fines depending on the income of the offender so, for example, the

---

1   'Significant modifications' included changing the seriousness indicators or the entry levels for some of the offences.

suggested fine for the offence of falsely obtaining electricity was within the range £120 and £300. Bench guidelines for two other courts set a norm for people on average income which could be reduced by up to half for people on low incomes or doubled for the better off.

All but one of the courts followed the recommendations of the Best Practice Guidance issued by the Lord Chancellor's Department (1990) to obtain information about their income on means forms. (The other court relied on questions in court.) The forms ask for information on income and regular outgoings. In cases where there was no information on the means of the defendant (e.g. because he or she pleaded guilty by letter) the court would assume that the defendant had an 'average income'.

> *If they fail to complete the form, we assume that they can pay the going rate, whatever that may be.*

Sentencers recognised that this could result in low-income defendants being fined more than they might be but felt that it would not be practicable to adjourn in every case to obtain means information. If the offender was unable to pay the fine, it could be reassessed at a means enquiry.

> *The only thing that you can do is hope that they will be shocked enough to come into the office to sort something out.*

Fining low-income offenders – magistrates' views

Where there was no local guidance on the size of fines for people on low incomes, magistrates would often set the maximum at what they believed the defendant could afford to pay over a year. As magistrates assumed that the maximum weekly amount that a person receiving benefits could afford to pay was between £3 and £5 a week, the maximum fine for unemployed offenders was normally between £150 and £250.

Fining people on low incomes for driving without insurance and not having a TV licence was felt to pose special problems. In order to create a deterrent, it was important that the offender did not benefit from the offence, so any fine had to be more than the cost of car insurance or a TV licence. However, this could lead to fines which were beyond the means of the offenders although for motor insurance cases penalty points can be an additional punishment. One magistrate said:

> *We all resent having to fine people very low amounts for no insurance. We're all sitting in court, having paid our dues, and they*

> *are taking a chance and getting away with it. If they are on income support, how can they afford to own a car?*

Unfortunately, allowing low-income offenders to 'get away with it' was seen as unavoidable if the Court is to set fines that can be enforced. As one Justices' Clerk said:

> *It might be galling that the fine is cheaper than paying for motor insurance, but, at the end of the day, you can't get blood out of a stone. If you are to have any chance at all of enforcing the fine, you have to set the level of the fine that they can pay in the first instance. That is the difficult bit.*

In contrast, magistrates sometimes regretted having to impose fines for not having a TV licence which were heavy in relation to the offender's income:

> *By imposing the fine* [for no TV licence] *you are making that person into a criminal. My worry is that magistrates' courts are putting people into a situation where they are going to a loan shark to pay a fine and making a bigger problem.*

Fining the wealthy – magistrates' views

There were mixed views about increasing fines for more wealthy offenders:

> *A fine is a punishment and someone who is very wealthy and given a small fine, it would mean nothing to them. But to someone who hasn't got much money, the same financial penalty would be a big punishment. That's why I think that we have got to be flexible.*

The fact that the wealthy received larger fines was also seen as increasing the credibility of the fine:

> *You get footballers for example. The man in the street knows what their wages are. When they get caught speeding or drunk and disorderly the fine has to pull up the general public with a jerk so they think 'I'm not doing that'.*

However, other magistrates did not support the principle of bigger fines for wealthy people:

> *I don't think that someone is likely to be punished because he's got extra money. I think that what we're doing is imposing a realistic fine and scaling it down because of lack of income. A wealthy person doesn't need it scaling down so he gets the realistic fine.*

These contrasting opinions meant that wealthy offenders could receive very different fines at different courts as the size of fine imposed depends largely upon the views of the magistrates at that court.

The conditional discharge

A conditional discharge is recorded as a conviction, and if the offender commits another offence during the period of the discharge, they will be liable to be sentenced for the offence on which the conditional discharge was imposed as well as the new offence. A fifth (21%) of offenders who received a conditional discharge were also ordered to pay compensation. In interviews, magistrates said that the value of the conditional discharge was that it deterred the offender from committing more offences during the currency of the order. It was frequently described as a *'warning'* or likened to the *'Sword of Damocles hanging over the offender'*. Conditional discharges were seen as particularly suitable for first offenders. Figure 5.5 shows that 17 per cent of first offenders received a conditional discharge compared to 10 per cent of those with previous convictions. As one magistrate said:

> *Sometimes you just feel that a conditional discharge might help because it just keeps something hanging over them; they have to remember that, if they are tempted again, there could be trouble. A fine, it's all finished, it's done.*

Figure 5.5: Factors associated with receiving a conditional discharge rather than another sentence (Source: Magistrates' courts survey)

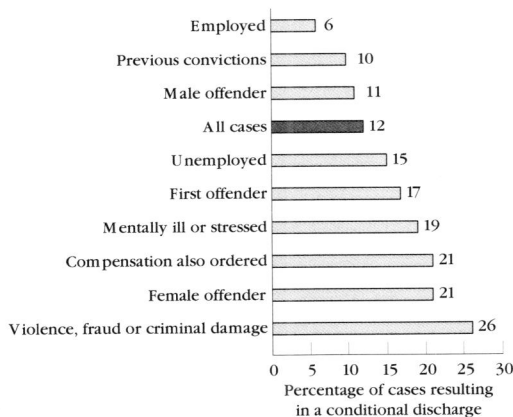

Category	Value
Employed	6
Previous convictions	10
Male offender	11
All cases	12
Unemployed	15
First offender	17
Mentally ill or stressed	19
Compensation also ordered	21
Female offender	21
Violence, fraud or criminal damage	26

Percentage of cases resulting in a conditional discharge

Magistrates said that they often struggled to decide whether a conditional discharge or a fine was more appropriate. One sentencer explained that the choice between a fine and a conditional discharge:

> *probably causes the most disagreement in the retirement room. You have to decide what you want to achieve because with a conditional discharge you might want to achieve something entirely different to the fine. The fine might just be a punitive thing or it might be that they've had similar offences before. A conditional discharge may be a one-off but there is a lot of discussion between a fine and a conditional discharge and I think that only by looking at what you want to achieve are you able to decide.*

Frequently magistrates were unable to say how they came to a decision between the two options at this level of sentencing. Some said that, having considered the facts of the offence and the circumstances of the offender, the decision was *'intuitive'*. Another said:

> *you marry the offender, the mitigating circumstances and the offence. You put all of these together and you come up with a decision. Its an art rather than a science.*

Stress and mental health problems were associated with a conditional discharge (Figure 5.5) [2].

A conditional discharge was received by 21 per cent of women compared to just 11 per cent of men and there was still a significant difference when the differences in employment status were controlled for. Other research found this reflects in part, the problem of fining women who did not work and so did not have any income of their own; fining them would penalise the 'innocent' wage-earning partner. Secondly, women often had primary responsibility for children and so magistrates did not want to take much-needed income away from the family (Gelsthorpe and Loukes, 1997). Sentencers did not seem to apply the same considerations to fathers.

The absolute discharge

The only effect of an absolute discharge is to mark the conviction. In 1995 absolute discharges accounted for just under two per cent of all sentences in magistrates' courts. Less than one per cent of the cases in the sample (26) resulted in an absolute discharge, two-thirds of which were motoring offences. The majority were first, or at most second-time, offenders.

---

2 Cases that resulted in a conditional discharge were more likely to have had a pre-sentence report than those which were fined. Magistrates often requested a pre-sentence report in case when they suspected after hearing about the case in court that the offender may have particular difficulties: in total a pre-sentence report was available in 16% of cases which resulted in a conditional discharge compared with 5% of those who received a fine.

There were five circumstances in which magistrates said absolute discharges might be appropriate, of which four were reflected in our sample.

Strict liability cases

Magistrates said that the most frequent situation where they would consider an absolute discharge was where the offender was technically guilty but had not intended to commit the offence. In one such case, a 34-year-old man was convicted of driving without insurance. His solicitor explained that, because he could neither hear nor write, he had problems communicating with his insurance company and so accidentally found himself without insurance. In another case of driving without insurance, the defendant explained that she mistakenly believed that she was named on her husband's insurance policy and was insured to drive any vehicle. Magistrates accepted that she had made a genuine mistake. In a speeding case, the defendant admitted the offence, but told the court that his car had a defective speedometer which meant that he did not know how fast he was travelling.

Defendant is not culpable

There were two cases in the sample in which the defendants' mental health meant that magistrates either considered that they were not really culpable or that punishing the offender might interfere with treatment. In one case, the defendant was convicted of possession of an offensive weapon (a knife) in a public place. He had a history of mental health problems, but was receiving treatment and was progressing well. Magistrates encouraged the defendant to carry on with the treatment. In the other case, the offender was convicted of making obscene phone calls and failing to surrender to bail. He had mental health problems and was receiving hospital treatment.

As an administrative measure

Absolute discharges can be used as an administrative measure where an offender has been convicted of a number of charges at a single instance, but the court does not wish to impose penalties on them all (Wasik, 1993). For example, in a case where an offender pleaded guilty to a range of road traffic offences, the court heard that the defendant had already been disqualified from driving for six months by another court for similar offences earlier that day. The second court decided not to penalise him further.

To register disapproval of the decision to prosecute or of the investigation

An absolute discharge can be used if the court wants to register disapproval of police methods or the decision to prosecute (Wasik, 1993). As one magistrate said:

> *The CPS think very carefully before bringing a case. I wouldn't think that you get many cases that would attract an absolute discharge because the CPS would sort them out before they came to court. An absolute discharge is a sign that a prosecution shouldn't have been brought. You have to use your common sense. The fact that there are very few absolute discharges maybe says that the CPS are getting it right.*

We had no examples in this study.

As the least severe penalty

There were a few examples in the sample where an absolute discharge appeared to be given because the offence was not felt to merit anything more. Two cases involved women convicted of shoplifting where the stolen goods had been recovered. One of the women was a first offender, the other had only one previous conviction. Magistrates accepted that their offences arose because the women were mothers of young children coping on low incomes. (More often such cases resulted in a conditional discharge.)

6 The use of compensation orders

The proportion of sentenced offenders ordered to pay compensation has declined since 1990 (Figure 6.1) Compensation was most frequently awarded for offences of violence and criminal damage (Figure 6.2). Other property offences (burglary, theft and deception) were much less likely to result in compensation. Motoring cases rarely involved compensation; those that did usually involved damage caused by an offender without insurance or failure to report an accident. Several magistrates said that they found it difficult to award compensation in motoring cases because only a small amount of damage to a car will cost hundreds of pounds to repair which is beyond most offenders' means. In two courts magistrates said that they got round this problem by making a compensation order to the value of the excess on the victim's insurance policy, sometimes including an amount to compensate for higher insurance premiums in future.

Figure 6.1: Proportion of sentenced offenders ordered to pay compensation in magistrates' courts 1984-1996 (Indictable offences only) (Source: Criminal Statistics 1996)

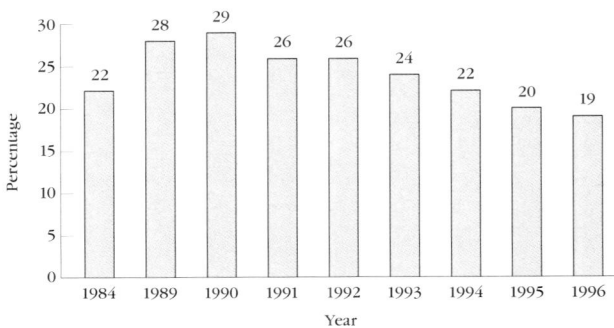

Figure 6.2: Proportion of cases where compensation awarded Non-custodial sentences only (Source: Magistrates' courts survey)

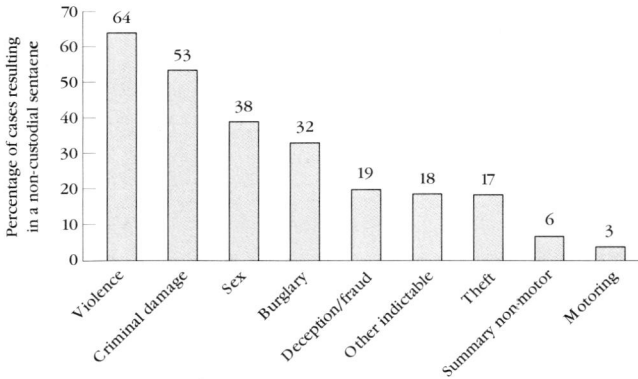

Compensation and other sentences

In less than one per cent of the sample was a compensation order given as the only sentence. Although it is possible to combine a compensation order with any other sentence, Figure 6.3 shows that compensation was rarely awarded at the same time as a custodial sentence. This accords with the principle in Inwood (1974) that it will normally be undesirable to have a compensation order hanging over the offender when they leave prison. The CJA 1991 required a court, when imposing a suspended sentence, to actively consider whether a fine or compensation order should be imposed as well. There were very few suspended sentences in this sample but *Criminal Statistics* 1994 show that 31 per cent of offenders who received a suspended sentence were also required to pay compensation.

Figure 6.3: Proportionate use of compensation by sentence (Source: Magistrates' courts survey)

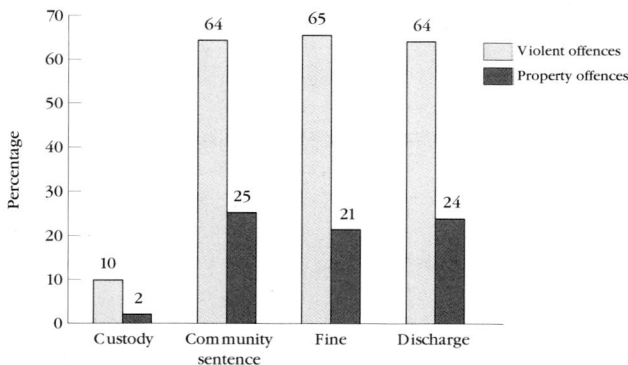

Compensation for personal injury

In violent offences, compensation was least likely to be awarded where the offence took place in a 'domestic' setting where the victim was either the partner of the offender or another family member although even in these cases 50 per cent included compensation (Table 6.1). Magistrates said in interviews that they were sometimes reluctant to award compensation which could be unhelpful in domestic situations where the offender and victim had a financial relationship (whether living in the same household or where one partner was paying maintenance to the other). One magistrate said:

> ....there is no way in which you will get a husband to pay compensation to his wife.

Compensation was awarded in around three-quarters of cases where the victim was not a family member or the partner of the offender. Magistrates said that they occasionally refrained from awarding compensation where the victim and offender were friends because it could revive tensions.

Table 6.1 Compensation by relationship to the offender (Violence cases which did not result in immediate custody only)[1]

	n	percentage of cases where compensation awarded
Friend or acquaintance	23	78
Stranger	30	77
Police officer /other in position of authority[2]	16	75
Partner / other family member	42	50
Total	111	67

Note:
1. Custodial sentences were excluded because compensation was rarely awarded. Information was missing for 10 cases.
2. Includes store detectives, paramedics etc.

Magistrates were also more likely to award compensation where the victim had suffered some identifiable injury as against where they had been frightened or upset but not physically hurt. Unlike property offences, where there is often a good estimate of the value of the loss, it can be very difficult to attach a value to injuries or to fear and distress. Newburn (1988) identified the difficulty of fixing a monetary value to an injury as the main reason for not awarding compensation where there has been harm or distress. The Home Office issued a circular in 1988 which used figures drawn up by the Criminal Injuries Compensation Board to provide guidance on the sum to be awarded for a range of injuries. Recommendations for different levels of injury are included in the Magistrates' Association guidelines; currently the recommended compensation for a bruise is £75, for a facial scar which leaves the victim permanently disfigured, £750, and for a broken arm, £2,500. Magistrates in all 12 courts said that they referred to the guidelines when they awarded compensation for injury. However, in two courts it was argued that the amounts suggested by the guidelines were high in relation to the income of many offenders and often had to be reduced substantially:

> *If you are thinking of compensating someone for an assault on a neighbour for example, the guidelines might suggest that you should be awarding £300-£400. That's totally out of touch with people's means.*

The Magistrates' Association guidelines suggest that compensation for minor injuries should be between £30 and £400. Compensation for more serious injuries is suggested at between £300 and £500. Average awards recorded in this study included £30 for grazes and £375 for sprains. Victims who had more serious injuries did receive somewhat more compensation: the average amount awarded for a minor injury was £136, while for a more serious injury the average award was £169. Where the victim had not been physically hurt in the offence and the magistrates were compensating the victim for distress or inconvenience, the average award was £94.

Reasons for not awarding compensation

The 1988 Criminal Justice Act required magistrates to state the reason for not awarding compensation in open court. Table 6.2 shows that this rarely happened and so the circumstances in which they would consider not awarding compensation were also pursued in group interviews.

The reason most frequently stated in court for not awarding compensation in property offences was because all the stolen goods had been recovered and restored to the owner (Table 6.2). In four per cent of violent offences and three per cent of property offences that fact that the offender was in prison was given as the reason for not awarding compensation.

In a small number of violent (5%) and property (7%) offences, magistrates stated that compensation was not awarded because it had not been requested by the victim. In most cases, the issue of compensation was not addressed during the hearing. However, this was no doubt also the case in most instances where the issue of compensation did not arise at all. Previous research found that the absence of any request for compensation was the most common reason for not awarding it (Moxon, Corkery and Hedderman, 1992: viii). Although the court can make a compensation order whether or not it is raised in the hearing, that study found that sentencers were often reluctant to do so in the absence of any evidence that the victim was seeking compensation coupled with information to help them assess how much would be appropriate.

Table 6.2 Reasons for not awarding compensation stated in court (Violence and property offences only) (Magistrates' Court survey)

	Violence		Property offences[1]	
	n	% cases	n	% cases
No reason given	114	80	445	70
All stolen goods were recovered	N/A	N/A	97	15
Other reason	14	10	17	3
Compensation was not sought by the victim	7	5	44	7
Offender in prison	6	4	20	3
Low income of the offender	2	1	22	3
Recompense made by offender prior to sentencing	2	1	4	0.6
No information on the value of loss/injury was provided	0	0	5	1
Offender paying other compensation orders	0	0	1	0.2
Offender ill and unable to pay	0	0	1	0.2
Total number of cases[2]	143		640	

Note:
1. Excludes property offences which did not involve loss to the victim.
2. Magistrates' could give more than one reason.

All the magistrates who took part in the group interviews emphasised the importance of compensation and saw it as a suitable punishment for offenders as well as serving the interests of victims:

> *I like the use of compensation because I think that nothing hurts the offender more than having to pay money to the victim.*

> *I think that compensation is a better punishment than a fine, and it probably irks the offender more because they know that money is actually going to the person they slugged in the eye or whatever. That must be a rather sobering thought.*

Despite the requirement to give priority to compensation over fines, there were a number of cases where magistrates stated in court that the value of the compensation order was reduced but they went on to impose a fine or order for costs. Almost two-thirds (65%) of offenders in cases where the value of the compensation was reduced, were ordered to pay a fine and/or costs. Even in cases where the reason for the compensation being reduced was specifically stated to be because the offender could not afford to pay more, 36 per cent of offenders were ordered to pay a fine and/or costs.

The main reason that magistrates' gave for not awarding compensation was the low income of the offender which meant they were not in a position to pay compensation (Figure 6.4).

Forty per cent of offenders in work and 27 per cent of unemployed offenders convicted of a violent or property offence and not imprisoned were ordered to pay compensation:

Figure 6.4: Reasons given by magistrates for not awarding compensation (Source: Interviews in 12 magistrates' courts)

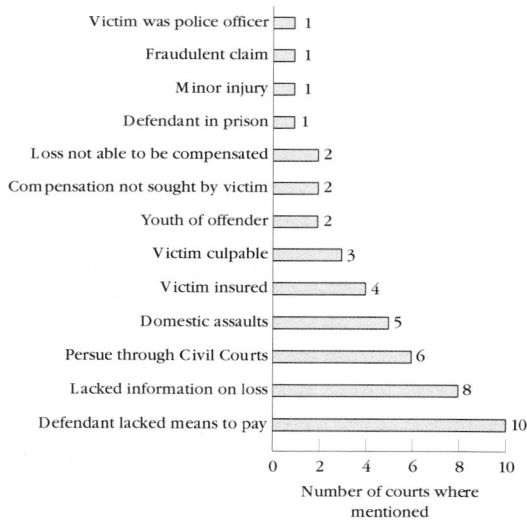

However, once made, a compensation order cannot be remitted without the victim's agreement. As one magistrate put it, *'unlike fines, you only have one chance to get it right'.* As discussed earlier (in the context of fines) magistrates felt £3 to £5 a week was a realistic maximum for unemployed offenders.

You have to look at their means and what would be a reasonable sum to award. Ninety-odd per cent of people when sentenced are on benefit and the DSS won't deduct more than £2.30 or £2.40. You have to look at what they can afford and, all right, we might stretch it over two years for compensation, but at the end of the day they are not going to be paying a large amount.

We are dealing with defendants who are very inadequate financially and, although you would like to make an award, it is impossible because they don't have the means to pay.

The Court of Appeal has ruled that fines and compensation might properly be paid over a period of up to three years.[1] Financial penalties in the magistrates' court are *normally* set at a level where payment within 12 months is possible. In appropriate cases (for example, where there is a compelling case for adequate compensation) this may be longer.

Where the amount of loss or injury merited compensation which was substantially more than the offender could pay, stipendiary magistrates in one area made the point that compensation which did not reflect what had happened could be viewed as derisory by the victim and they felt that this could bring the criminal justice system into disrepute.

The second reason stated for not awarding compensation was lack of information. This was a common problem with property offences. Even where information was available, the defence often disputed the amount and magistrates needed solid evidence – such as an invoice or receipt – but often only had a statement of what was lost:

How many times have you sat in a court and the defence has objected to a value in a charge and the CPS has said, 'Can we amend that to 'value unknown'? The minute they do that, that takes out the compensation.

I can think of at least one occasion where I refused compensation, or at least not to the amount that was claimed, because there was no real evidence. The estimate that was before us seemed to be one of these that a mate had written for him, so I refused to accept it.

The Court of Appeal[2] has cautioned sentencers against 'simply plucking a figure out of the air', although some magistrates said that they were sometimes prepared to use their own judgement about what would be a reasonable sum.

In this part of the world we are all short of money and we are all a lot of 'do-it-yourself-ers'. We have a jolly good idea of how much it

---

1   Swan (1984) 6 Cr App R (S) 22 per Kilner Brown J.
2   Oliver (1989) 11 CR App R (S) 10.

costs, say, to replace a window, because we have personal experience of it.

People come to court and just don't have the written information and feel that they can just say, 'He did £150 worth of damage'. We either adjourn for more information or work out what would be reasonable.

Although magistrates could adjourn a case for the Crown Prosecution Service to get further information, they were reluctant to impose further delays – especially as there was no guarantee that the information would be forthcoming.

The need to provide full information on injury or loss has been underlined in two Court of Appeal judgements[3] where it was held that, if a victim's injuries are disputed, compensation should not be awarded unless evidence is produced to prove the injuries alleged by the prosecution. The Victim's Charter (Home Office, 1990) put responsibility on the police to provide information for compensation. It said that:

The police should ensure that they know what loss or injury the victim has suffered – to pass on to the CPS and court if someone is charged, in order to ensure that no victim loses their right to compensation by oversight.

The Charter also says that victims should be asked to keep records to facilitate a compensation claim. However, it is clear that there are many cases in which compensation cannot be awarded because the courts do not have good enough information.

Pursuing losses through the Civil Court

As an alternative to compensation, it is open to victims to pursue claims through the civil courts. Courts sometimes draw the victim's attention to this option:

The victim has a right to civil action and I content myself that, if he has won in this court, that will stand him in good stead in the county court. That court may be better trained to deal with it.

However, magistrates said it was not practical to expect victims to go through this potentially lengthy civil process.

---

3   R v Chorley Justices, ex parte Jones (1990) 754 JP 420 and R v Horsham Justices, ex parte Richards (1985), 2 All E.R. 1114.

Victim's culpability

If the victim was partly to blame magistrates said that they would not award compensation. An example in which this might occur would be a street brawl where as one magistrate said:

> *I think that you are less sympathetic to a compensation claim where the victim was as much to blame as the assailant.*

7 Sentencing patterns of lay and stipendiary magistrates

The first salaried magistrates were introduced in London in the mid-eighteenth century. Twenty-seven 'police magistrates'[1] were appointed in 1792 to sit in seven police offices (later renamed police courts). Lay justices did not disappear in London but were restricted to working on petty crime and administrative matters such as licensing. Lay justices sat in separate courts and were serviced by different staff (Seago, Walker and Wall, 1995: 12). In 1813 the first Provincial Stipendiary Magistrate was appointed in Manchester and the Municipal Corporations Act 1835 required local authorities to petition the Home Office and state their reasons for appointing a stipendiary.[2] Outside London, stipendiaries were only appointed in exceptional circumstances. The number of stipendiaries in London remained constant for over a century although lay magistrates were gradually reintroduced into criminal business; for example, the 1920 Juvenile Courts (Metropolis) Act allowed a bench of two lay magistrates sitting with a stipendiary and from 1933 no stipendiary was required at all. Lay magistrates regained full jurisdiction in the 1964 Administration of Justice Act.

The current position

In the past 20 years the number of stipendiary magistrates has grown. The Administration of Justice Act 1973 allowed the Lord Chancellor to appoint up to 40 provincial stipendiary magistrates and 60 metropolitan stipendiaries. There was no immediate increase in the number of stipendiaries but since the Lord Chancellor's Department published criteria for the appointment of stipendiaries in the provinces in 1988, the number has increased from seven to 39 (at October 1995). There are over 30,000 lay magistrates. Seago et al. (1995:14) attribute the increase in stipendiaries in part to the increase in court business and to the fact that the work of magistrates has become more complex as increasingly serious offences have been reclassified as summary. Expectations of training have also been increased so that lay magistrates must be able not only to attend long and

---

1.   Their title was changed to 'metropolitan stipendiary magistrate' in 1949.
2.   This was extended to less populated areas in the 1863 Stipendiary Magistrates Act.

complex court sittings but also lengthy training sessions. This has led to difficulties in recruiting a sufficient number of lay justices in some areas. Stipendiaries are also seen as being quicker and concerns about efficiency and delays have led to more courts appointing stipendiaries or using temporary stipendiary magistrates to clear backlogs.

Not many courts have full-time stipendiary magistrates. Outside London, stipendiaries are concentrated in metropolitan areas although some Shire counties such as Hampshire, Norfolk and Shropshire have peripatetic stipendiaries who sit in courts throughout the county. Some magistrates' courts share a stipendiary who will work for a week at a time in each court. Temporary visits are also possible; in 1994, 59 courts that did not have a permanent stipendiary magistrate received at least one visit from a stipendiary.

Although stipendiary magistrates play an important role in the criminal justice system, there has been very little research on them[3]. This chapter compares the sentencing patterns of stipendiary and lay justices. As the position of stipendiary magistrates is somewhat different in London to elsewhere, this is considered separately where appropriate.

Stipendiary and lay magistrates

Figure 7.1 shows that stipendiary magistrates both in London and elsewhere were more likely to sentence an offender to custody than lay justices; the latter made more use of community sentences. However, on the raw figures, the proportion of offenders sentenced to custody by provincial stipendiary magistrates was almost twice that sentenced to custody by stipendiaries in London.

Figure 7.1: Sentencing patterns of lay and stipendiary magistrates (Source: Magistrates' courts survey)

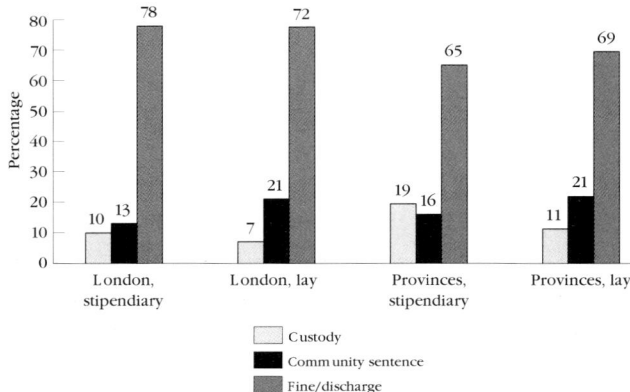

---

3.   The most recent research on stipendiaries is Seago, Walker and Wall (1995).

Table 7.1 shows that stipendiary magistrates imposed custody more often than lay justices in cases involving violent, sexual, property or motoring offences.

Table 7.1 Proportionate use of custody: lay and stipendiary magistrates by offence

Offence type	London stipendiary % custody	London lay % custody	Provinces stipendiary % custody	Provinces lay % custody
Violent and sexual	17	5	31	16
Property	20	8	21	11
Other indictable	2	2	2	4
Summary – non-monitoring	3	4	7	4
Summary – monitoring	13	9	27	14
Total percentage	9	7	18	10
Total number	577	925	309	1,191

However, the workload of stipendiary magistrates is often very different from lay magistrates; for example, where a case involves a complex legal argument or is likely to last several days, it is often best dealt with by a stipendiary. This makes comparisons difficult. The statistical technique of logistic regression was used to disentangle the effect of the type of magistrate from other key factors, namely the sex of the offender, nature and number of offences, whether the offender had previous convictions or any similar convictions and whether they were subject to any other court orders at the time of the offence.[4]

This analysis found that the type of magistrate had an independent effect on the outcome and confirmed that lay magistrates used custody less. However other variables – the offence type, whether the offender was subject to a court order at the time of the offence and the number of offences for which they were sentenced – had a bigger effect on the outcome.

Influence of stipendiary magistrates on lay magistrates' sentencing practice

Stipendiary magistrates frequently take part in training the lay justices in their areas and so might be expected to foster a common approach. However, the stipendiaries interviewed did not believe that they followed

---

4   The best fitting model did not distinguish between stipendiary magistrates in London and elsewhere. (Appendix C, Table C.9).

the guidelines as closely as their lay colleagues. They felt that lay magistrates sometimes lacked confidence to depart from the guidelines whereas stipendiaries felt more able to do so because of their legal background and lifetime of working in courts. The sentencing practices of three groups of magistrates were compared to see if there were differences in sentencing: stipendiaries, lay magistrates who sit in courts where there are stipendiary magistrates and lay magistrates who sit in courts without stipendiaries. Figure 7.2 indicates that there is evidence of an increase in severity of sentencing by lay magistrates in courts with stipendiaries.

Figure 7.2: Proportionate use of custody by different types of magistrates (Source: Magistrates' courts survey)

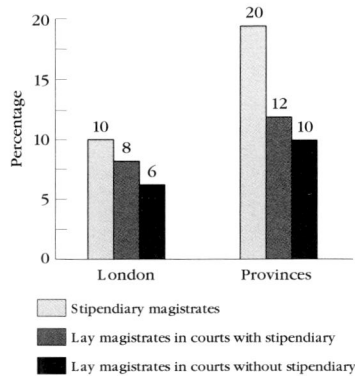

Legend:
Stipendiary magistrates
Lay magistrates in courts with stipendiary
Lay magistrates in courts without stipendiary

It is difficult to draw any firm conclusions from this limited evidence, but it appears that the lay justices in London sentence similarly to stipendiaries while in the provincial areas stipendiaries are much more severe than lay justices. This may reflect the differing role of stipendiary magistrates: within London, stipendiaries have a long established role in criminal matters and may take a more central role in the training of magistrates (Seago et al. 1995 :13). Provincial stipendiaries do not have such a history of working alongside the lay justices and may just be working in the court for a short period if they are appointed on a peripatetic or shared basis.

Part 3

The Crown Court

Claire Flood-Page

8 Custody decisions in the Crown Court

Apart from the type of offence, research has consistently found that criminal record is the most important factor in custody decisions (see, for example, Moxon, 1988). In this study, previous criminal history was measured by three variables: the number of previous convictions, whether the offender had committed similar offences in the past and whether they were subject to a court order at the time of the current offence.

Previous criminal record

Figure 8.1 shows that, for first offenders, those under 21 were less likely to receive a custodial sentence than those aged 21 and over. For those with previous convictions there was little difference (Figure 8.2). Offenders under 21 were slightly more likely to receive a community penalty than their older peers: in particular they were more likely to receive probation or a combination order. A higher proportion of offenders aged 21 and over were fined.

Figure 8.1: Sentencing of first offenders by age (Source: Crown Court survey)

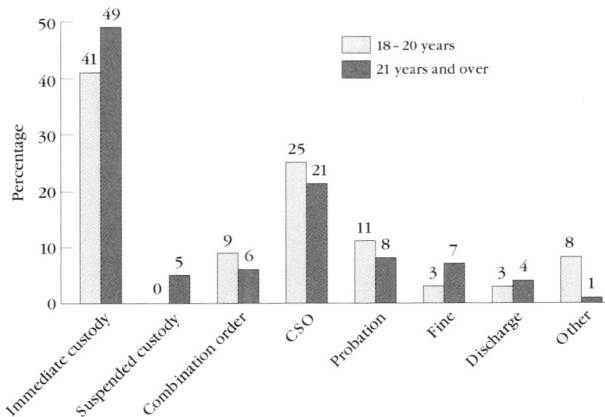

Figure 8.2: Sentencing of offenders with previous convictions by age (Source: Crown Court survey)

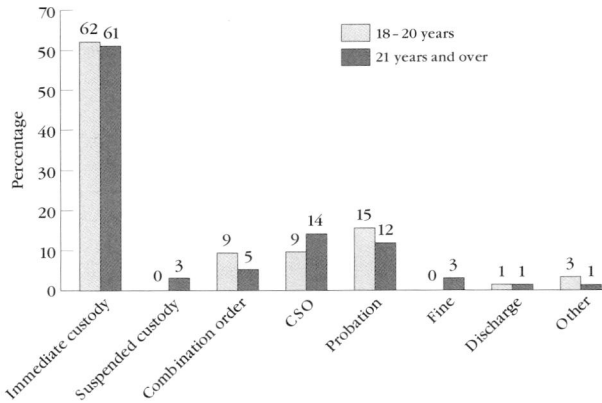

Figure 8.3 shows that the proportion of people imprisoned increased steadily as the number of previous convictions rose: 47 per cent of first offenders were imprisoned compared to 60 per cent of those with between two and five previous convictions and 65 per cent of those with more than five convictions. Of those with previous convictions for a similar offence, 63 per cent received a custodial sentence. compared to 60 per cent of those where previous convictions were for different kinds of offence: this was not statistically significant and may have been due to chance.

Figure 8.3: Proportionate use of custody by number of previous convictions (Source: Crown Court survey)

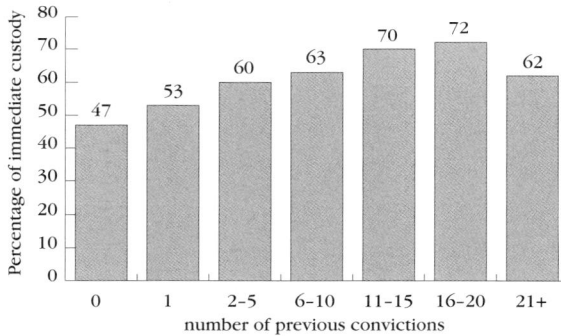

Response to previous court orders

Two-thirds of offenders (68%) who were subject to a court order when they committed the current offence were sentenced to custody (Figure 8.4). Thirteen per cent of the sample were subject to a community sentence at the time that they committed the current offence and almost three-quarters of these received a custodial sentence. Similarly, three-quarters of those who were on bail or were released on licence at the time of the current offence received a custodial sentence. Interestingly, in contrast to other breaches, being in breach of a suspended sentence did not increase the risk of custody: only 55 per cent of those who were subject to a suspended sentence received custody. Although a new offence would not represent a breach of the community penalty, offending while subject to a conditional discharge or suspended sentence does constitute a breach and the offender may be re-sentenced for the earlier offence as well as the current one.

Figure 8.4: Proportionate use of custody by whether subject to a court order (Source: Crown Court survey)

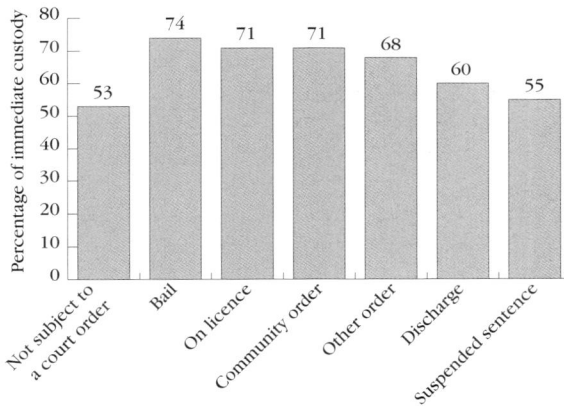

Type of court order to which offender subject when they committed current crime

Remand status

Offenders who had been remanded in custody prior to sentencing were more than twice as likely to receive a custodial sentence as those on bail: the figure was 86 per cent and 41 per cent respectively. However, factors which affect the sentencing decision overlap with those which influence remand decisions; for example, both are influenced by the seriousness of the offence and the defendant's criminal record. Figure 8.5 shows that, for both first offenders and those with previous convictions, those who had been remanded in custody prior to sentencing were more likely to receive a custodial sentence than those who had been on bail.

Figure 8.5: Proportionate use of custody by remand status at sentencing (Source: Crown Court survey)

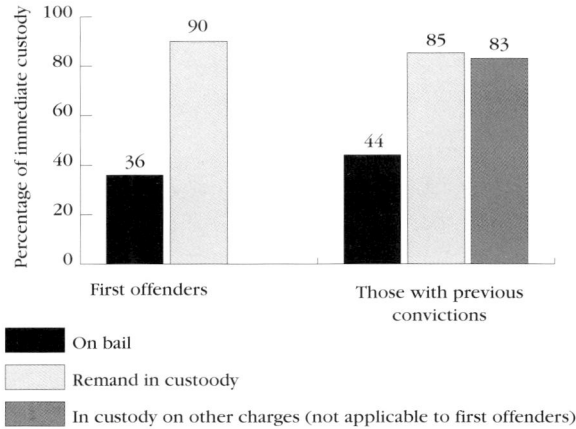

On bail

Remand in custoody

In custody on other charges (not applicable to first offenders)

Assessing the seriousness of the offence

Figure 8.6 shows that sexual offences and robbery most frequently resulted in custody (which is consistent with national statistics). Two-thirds of offenders charged with drugs offences and burglary were sent to prison. (The majority of drugs offences (77%) were for supplying drugs rather than simple possession.)

Figure 8.6: Proportionate use of immediate custody by offence type (Source: Crown Court survey)

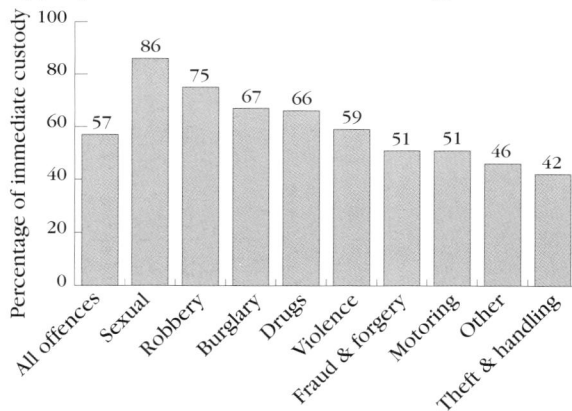

While Figure 8.6 gave an indication of which offence types were rated as most serious by the courts as measured by their use of custody, Figure 8.7 shows the mixture of offence- and offender-related factors which were associated with the use of custody. It shows, for example, the factors which determined whether or not a particular offence of theft would attract a custodial sentence, e.g. 72 per cent of cases where a breach of trust was involved received a custodial sentence.

Figure 8.7: Factors associated with the use of immediate custody (Source: Crown Court survey)

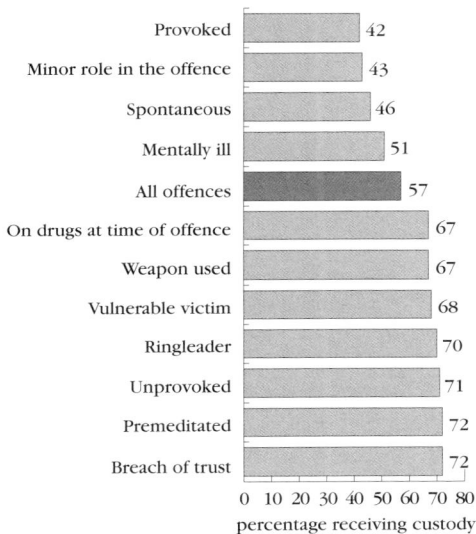

Immediate custody was more likely where the incident was unprovoked or premeditated, involved the use of a weapon, there was serious injury to the victim or the case involved a more substantial amount of loss or a vulnerable victim. Where more than one person is involved in an offence, their degree of involvement can be markedly different, and those who played a minor role were much less likely to receive a custodial sentence than ringleaders. Offenders who had abused a position of trust were particularly likely to receive a custodial sentence. Those who were mentally ill or under particular stress when they committed the offence were less likely to receive a prison term.

Figure 8.7 provides an overview. Some factors obviously apply only to property or only to violent offences.

Violence

Four out of five offenders convicted of manslaughter and 93 per cent of offenders sentenced for assault with intent to cause grievous bodily harm (Offences against the Person Act 1867 s18) received a custodial sentence compared to just over half (53%) of offenders convicted of a lesser violent offence.[1]

The three cases where an offender convicted of GBH s18 did not receive a custodial sentence were exceptional in various ways. In one example, a 30-year-old man was convicted of GBH s18 following an attack on a 68-year-old woman. He had a long record of previous convictions including some for violent offences. However the judge accepted that this incident had occurred while he was suffering from a drug-induced psychosis. He had since received treatment and his illness was controlled. He received a two-year probation order with a requirement that he continue to receive psychiatric treatment and live at a centre offering treatment for drug addiction.

The nature of the injury was recorded as was the relationship between the victim and offender and the sex and age of the victim.[2] Not surprisingly, there was a strong association between the type of injury and the likelihood of receiving a custodial sentence: all the cases where the victim died resulted in a custodial sentence as did three-quarters of cases where the victim had a fracture or received hospital treatment as an inpatient. Just over a third of violent offences where the victim was not injured resulted in a custodial sentence.

Premeditation made custody more likely (Figure 8.8). Many of the offences which were premeditated and which resulted in a serious injury were ones where the offender had allegedly 'taken the law into their own hands' and all resulted in a prison term. In one example, the victim was alleged to have raped the offender's wife. The attack on the victim caused such severe injuries that he was paralysed from the waist down. The offender had no previous convictions but received a six-year custodial sentence. The judge said it was a serious offence because 'the deliberate and callous attack had effectively brought an end to the victim's useful life'. In another case two co-defendants were convicted of two charges of assault causing grievous bodily harm with intent (GBH s18). The circumstances leading to the assaults were that one defendant had received complaints about a couple who rented a flat from him. He and his son took the law into their hands and assaulted

---

1   'Other violent offences' including GBH s20 (a less serious charge than GBH s18), assault causing actual bodily harm, wounding, as well as a range of other offences. Offences of murder were omitted from the sample because they attract a mandatory life sentence.

2   Observers were asked to record the ethnic appearance of the victim but this was difficult to do as it was rarely apparent from the case papers and the victim was not usually in court for sentencing.

the tenants. The male victim received a broken arm and head injuries and the woman also had head injuries. The landlord received a five-year prison term while his son, who had been 'egged on' by his father, got three years.

Figure 8.8: Violent offences. Factors associated with immediate custody (Source: Crown Court survey)

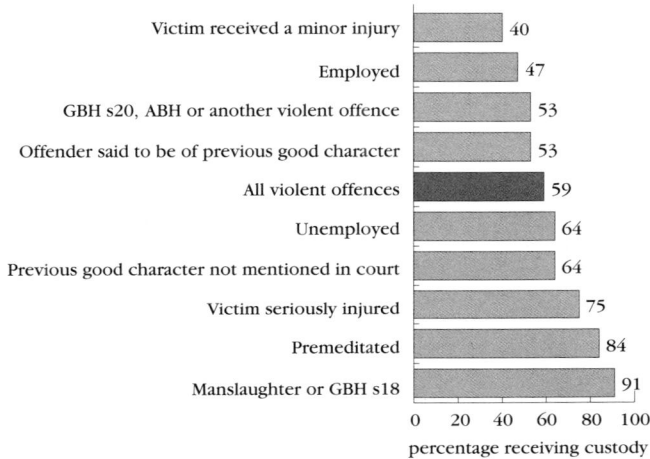

Sex offences

Eighty-six per cent of sex offenders received a custodial sentence, two were given suspended sentences, six were given community sentences, two were fined and one received a conditional discharge. Where the offender was given a conditional discharge, the offence had occurred five years previously and the offender had served a prison sentence for another similar offence in the meantime.

The offences resulting in a fine were both said by the judge to be at the 'less serious end of the scale'. A 32-year-old man was convicted after a trial of an indecent assault on a 16-year-old male. The victim was not physically injured in the assault. The offender was fined £1,000 and ordered to pay £500 compensation. He did not accept that he had committed an assault and so the probation service considered that he would not be suitable for community sentence.

Rape

Rape cases have been subject to particularly detailed guidance from the Court of Appeal. In Billam (1986)[3] the Court of Appeal made it clear that immediate custody is the appropriate sentence for rape in all but the most exceptional circumstances. Five years was given as the starting point for rape in contested cases without any mitigating or aggravating factors. There were 10 rape cases in the sample and all resulted in custody. The only defendant to receive less than five years was 16-years-old, and pleaded guilty. The victim was a 13-year-old girl who lived nearby and was known to the boy. In passing a 21 month sentence, the judge said that substantial credit had been given for the guilty plea which spared the young victim the ordeal of having to give evidence in court. The cases which resulted in the longest sentences had one or more of the following aggravating features:

* young victim

* abused trust of victim

* 'serial attacker' committing a number of rapes against different victims

* offence also involved violence or holding the victim prisoner

* offence was premeditated.

The case in the sample resulting in the longest sentence (11 years) involved a 27-year-old man who was convicted, following a trial, of rape and false imprisonment. This was his first offence. The victim was a stranger and had been subjected to an attack where she was threatened with a knife and raped several times.

Robbery

The maximum penalty for robbery is life imprisonment (Theft Act 1968 s.8(2)). Three-quarters of those sentenced for robbery received custodial sentences (most of the rest got a community sentence) with an average sentence of 3.7 years. Fifty-seven per cent of first offenders received a custodial sentence compared to 84 per cent of repeat offenders (Figure 8.9).

---

3   Billam (1986) 8 Cr App R (S) 48.

Figure 8.9: Robbery factors associated with the use of immediate custody (Source: Crown Court survey)

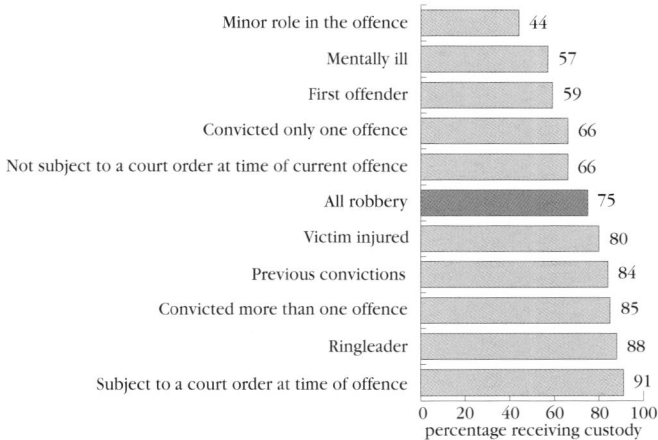

The Court of Appeal has placed robbery in three categories. Firstly, robbery of a bank or a post office or security vehicle in which L.J. Lawton said that the normal starting point for sentencing should be 15 years if firearms were carried but no injury was caused (Turner (1975) 61 Cr App R 67). Secondly, robbery of a sub-post office or shop will attract a substantial custodial sentence although perhaps below that of a 'first division' offence. The third category is street robbery or 'mugging'. The Court of Appeal has approved sentences of between two and five years for these offences (Wasik, 1993:329-330).

The cases in the study which attracted the longest custodial sentences (18 years) both involved armed robbery. In one of these cases the victim, a security guard, was shot in the leg. The offender had previous convictions for robbery and committed the offence after he had absconded from prison while on home leave.

Offenders who were mentally ill were less likely to be given a custodial sentence as were those under stress. In one example, the offender pleaded guilty to one charge of robbery and two charges of theft. In the robbery he, along with two co-defendants, had stolen a woman's handbag. She was not harmed and it was his first offence. The defence argued that he had been under considerable stress at the time of the offence and the judge agreed that he had made considerable progress since the offence; and felt that his continuing to live at the probation hostel, where he had been receiving support, might be the best way to prevent further offending. A two-year probation order with a special requirement that he live at a hostel was imposed.

Offenders with a co-defendant accounted for 43 per cent of the sample, and those who acted as ringleaders were twice as likely to receive a custodial sentence as those whose role in the offence was described as 'minor'. Eighty per cent of cases where the victim was injured resulted in custody.

Burglary

There is a guideline sentencing judgement giving general advice on the factors which should be taken into account in burglary cases[4]. Factors mentioned include whether the offence was premeditated, whether the house was occupied, the activities of the burglar within the house (e.g. whether there was any ransacking, vandalism or soiling) and the effect of the burglary upon the victim. In the sample, 64 per cent of burglary cases involved domestic burglary. Seventy-two per cent of domestic burglaries resulted in a prison sentence with an average length of 20.5 months. Fifty-seven per cent of commercial burglaries attracted custody, with an average sentence length of 18.5 months (Figure 8.10).

Figure 8.10: Burglary: Factors associated with immediate custody (Source: Crown Court survey)

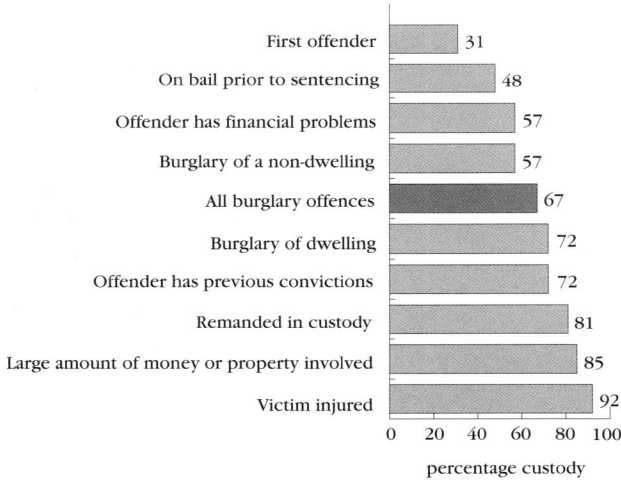

Factor	percentage custody
First offender	31
On bail prior to sentencing	48
Offender has financial problems	57
Burglary of a non-dwelling	57
All burglary offences	67
Burglary of dwelling	72
Offender has previous convictions	72
Remanded in custody	81
Large amount of money or property involved	85
Victim injured	92

The average loss in burglaries resulting in custody was £3,137 compared to an average of £1,076 in non-custody cases. Where the offender had serious financial difficulties, a custodial sentence was less likely.

---

4   Mussell (1990) 12 Cr App R (S) 612. Brewster (1998) 1 Cr App R (S) 181 also gives guidance on burglary. This research pre-dated that judgement.

Offenders in nine out of 10 cases of burglary or aggravated burglary where the victim was injured received a custodial sentence. In one example, the offender had broken into an occupied house and had stabbed the male householder; his wife had been hit in the face receiving cuts and bruises. No property was taken. The judge described this as 'a shocking offence leaving the victims terrified' and imposed a five year sentence. In a similar case, the 24-year-old offender was convicted of aggravated burglary and a number of other, less serious, charges. He had previously served a custodial sentence for burglary and was on bail at the time of the incident. The householder was badly injured and was blinded. The judge imposed a six-year sentence and said that, but for the offender's comparative youth and unstable background, a longer term would have been imposed.

Sentencing of repeat burglars

If implemented in full, the Crime (Sentences) Act will require a three-year mandatory minimum sentence for offenders convicted of their third offence of domestic burglary in all but the most exceptional circumstances.[5] The maximum sentence for domestic burglary remains at 14 years. A national sample of offenders sentenced at the Crown Court in 1993 to 1994 found that 75 per cent of domestic burglars with three or more previous convictions for burglary received a custodial sentence. The average sentence length in that sample was 18.9 months (Home Office, 1996:51-2). In our sample 75 per cent of domestic burglars with two or more previous convictions which included at least one previous conviction for burglary, received a custodial sentence. The average length of sentence was 22.6 months and 89 per cent of those sentenced to immediate custody received less than three years. By no means all of these burglars would have qualified for a mandatory three- year sentence under the new proposals as they may have had only one previous burglary conviction (our data did not record this), but it is clear that more repeat burglars will receive a custodial sentence and those that do will serve much longer periods in prison.

Theft

'Theft' includes such a wide range of offences that there is little formal guidance. In this study 46 per cent of theft cases were dealt with by a community sentence, and 42 per cent by immediate custody. Handling and theft involving a breach of trust were most likely to result in a custodial sentence (Figures 8.11 and 8.12).

---

5   The Home Secretary announced on 30th July 1997 that the implementation of these provisions would be considered in the light of resources and the Prison Service's capacity.

Figure 8.11: Proportionate use of custody for cases within the category 'theft' (Source: Crown Court survey)

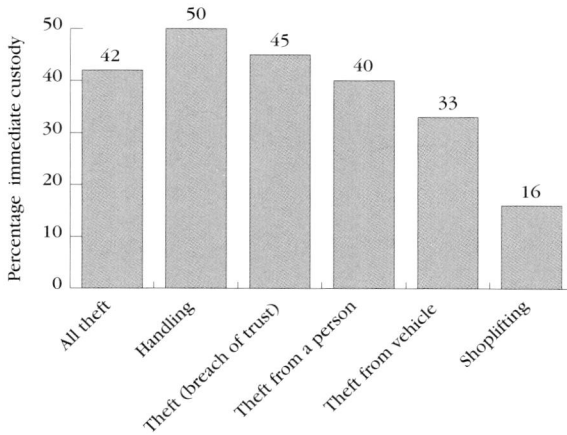

Figure 8.12: Theft offences. Factors associated with immediate custody (Source: Crown Court survey)

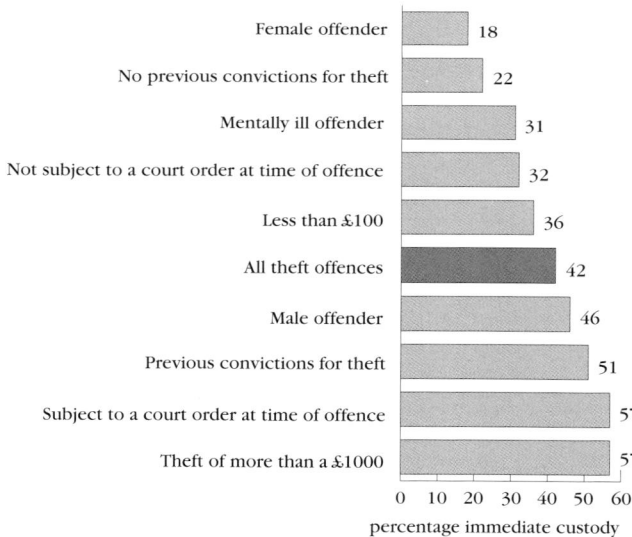

A key factor in handling cases was the extent to which the offender was seen as 'professional'.[6] In one such case, six men were charged with a number of offences of handling stolen goods which involved stealing cars from the street and changing their appearance in order to sell them. The three ringleaders received prison sentences of between two and three years: the three men who had played minor roles each received a CSO and were ordered to pay compensation of £1,000.

---

6   Khemiani (1981) 3 Cr App R (S) 208, Connor (1981) Cr App R (S) 225, Patel (1984) 6 Cr App R (S) 191 and Reader (1988) 10 Cr App R (S) 210.

Thirty-six per cent of thefts involving the loss of less than £100 resulted in custody compared to 57 per cent of those where the value of the property lost was more than £1,000. Where the offender was imprisoned for an offence involving a loss of less than £100, there were other aggravating factors: in every case but one the offender had a history of committing similar offences and, in five of the 11 cases, the offender was subject to an earlier court order when they had committed this offence. For example, in one case the offender was convicted of stealing a bottle of sparkling wine worth £12.99. He was also convicted of two charges of common assault arising from his struggling with the shop assistants who tried to stop him in the shop. He was drunk at the time of the offence. He had a long criminal record which included a number of similar offences, was subject to a probation order and was on bail at the time. He was given a seven-month sentence.

Theft involving the abuse of a postion of trust

The Court of Appeal indicated that where a person such as an accountant, solicitor, bank employee or postman has abused their position to steal a sizeable amount of money, custody will usually be appropriate.[7] In practice, custodial sentences are also imposed where the amount of money involved is fairly small but the abuse of position is particularly serious. In one example, the treasurer of a charity for blind people used his position to steal £600 from the charity's funds. Although he had repaid the money, he received a four-month sentence.

Just over half of the cases involving breach of trust did not receive a custodial sentence. One example was a female shop assistant who pleaded guilty to stealing supermarket vouchers worth £10,000 from her employer. The defence claimed that she was depressed at the time of the offence and had not actually used the vouchers. She had no previous convictions. In making a combination order, the judge said that, while custody was normally inevitable in this type of case, the exceptional personal mitigation meant that a community sentence was appropriate.

The above examples provide an interesting contrast. In neither case did the offender gain lasting benefit from the offence: in the first example the loss was repaid, while in the second the vouchers had not been used at the time of the arrest. The details of the cases explain the contrasting outcomes.

Moxon (1988) found that suspended sentences were often used in breach of trust cases. Since that study was undertaken in 1986, there has been a very sharp fall in the use of the suspended sentence overall in accordance with the CJA 1991. In this sample, eight per cent of theft offences which involved

---

7   Barrick (1985) 7 Cr App R (S) 142.

a breach of trust resulted in a suspended sentence compared to just three per cent of those convicted of other offences. There has been a marked shift to immediate custody and community sentences for such offences in the intervening years.

Drugs

The majority of drugs cases dealt with in the Crown Court involve supply rather than possession, and relate to the more serious Class A drugs such as heroin or cocaine rather than Class B or C drugs. Of the offenders convicted of supplying drugs, 76 per cent received a custodial sentence compared to 34 per cent of those convicted of possessing drugs (Figure 8.13). The average sentence for supplying drugs was 3.3 years compared to 18 months for possession. Among those convicted of possession 45 per cent received a community sentence, 13 per cent were fined and five per cent were given a conditional discharge.

Figure 8.13: Drug offences. Factors associated with immediate custody (Source: Crown Court survey)

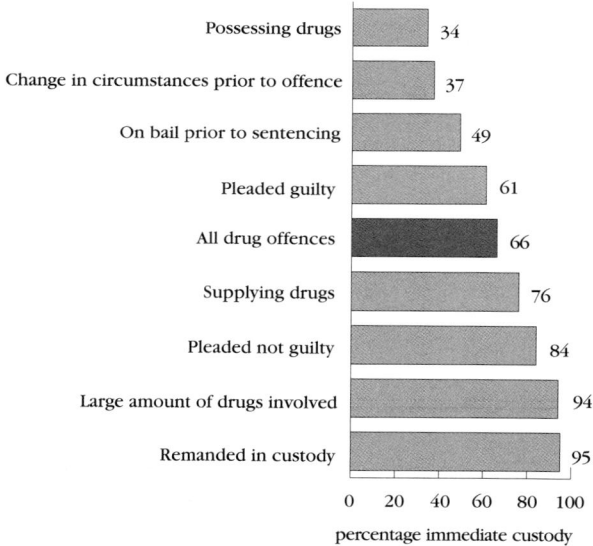

Factor	percentage immediate custody
Possessing drugs	34
Change in circumstances prior to offence	37
On bail prior to sentencing	49
Pleaded guilty	61
All drug offences	66
Supplying drugs	76
Pleaded not guilty	84
Large amount of drugs involved	94
Remanded in custody	95

Where large amounts of drugs were involved, a custodial sentence nearly always followed. Where their personal circumstances had changed since the offence, most typically because they had received treatment for addiction, custody was less likely. In one example, a 25-year-old woman was convicted of supplying Class A drugs. She had four sets of previous convictions, although these were not for drug offences. The judge said that the offence had occurred while she was addicted to drugs and living in a violent relationship which had now ended. She had a new home, had received treatment for her drug problem and had applied to regain custody of her child. She received a combination order made up of 15 months' probation and 45 hours of community service.

Length of sentence

In recent years the average sentence length has increased for most offence types: since 1985 the average length of sentence for men aged 21 and over has increased by almost five months from 17.3 months to 22.0 months in 1995. For women aged 21 and over it has risen from 12.5 months in 1985 to 17.7 in 1995.

Those convicted of robbery, drugs, violent and sexual offences received the longest sentences while those convicted of fraud and theft received the shortest (Figure 8.14).

Figure 8.14: Average sentence length
(Source: Crown Court survey)

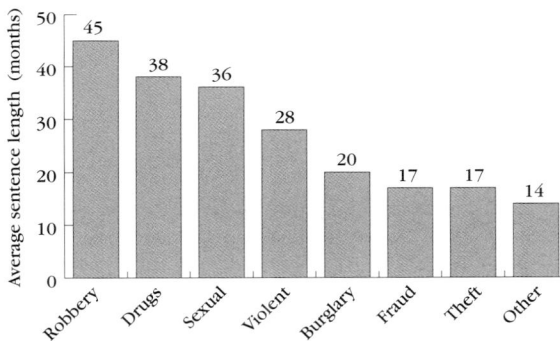

It is difficult to say by how much a particular factor increases the length of sentence because the mix of factors in each case is so variable. Aggravating factors – injury to a victim, that a weapon was used in the offence, that it was premeditated, that there was no expression of remorse or that the defendant was the ringleader – were associated with longer sentences (Figure 8.15). Some of these factors were shown in Figure 8.7 to be associated with a higher probability of receiving a custodial sentence in the first place.

Figure 8.16 shows the factors relating to the offender that were associated with receiving a sentence longer than 18 months. Offenders with special family responsibilities, or those that could show that their personal circumstances had changed since the offence, received shorter sentences. Unemployed offenders tended to receive longer sentences than those who had a job at the time that they were sentenced. Previously, it has been inferred that those who showed signs of a settled lifestyle and strong community ties, but whose offences were thought to require an immediate custodial sentence, were given shorter sentences to minimise the damage that being in prison would have on their domestic situation and future employment prospects (Moxon, 1988:32). Women were less likely than men to receive a custodial sentence longer than 18 months.

Figure 8.15: Offence-related factors associated with receiving more than 18-months custody (Source: Crown Court survey)

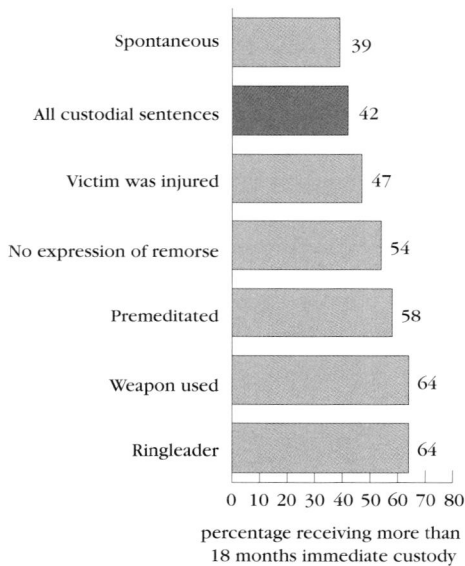

Factor	Percentage
Spontaneous	39
All custodial sentences	42
Victim was injured	47
No expression of remorse	54
Premeditated	58
Weapon used	64
Ringleader	64

0 10 20 30 40 50 60 70 80

percentage receiving more than
18 months immediate custody

88

**Figure 8.16: Offender-related factors associated with receiving
more than 18-months custody
(Source: Crown Court survey)**

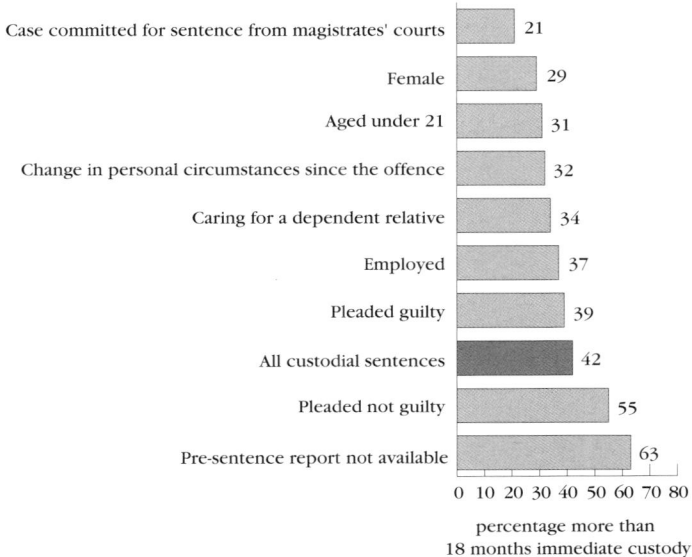

	percentage more than 18 months immediate custody
Case committed for sentence from magistrates' courts	21
Female	29
Aged under 21	31
Change in personal circumstances since the offence	32
Caring for a dependent relative	34
Employed	37
Pleaded guilty	39
All custodial sentences	42
Pleaded not guilty	55
Pre-sentence report not available	63

0 10 20 30 40 50 60 70 80

percentage more than
18 months immediate custody

Younger offenders tended to receive shorter sentences. Cases where there
was a pre-sentence report were more likely to result in a shorter sentence.
More detailed analysis has confirmed (Charles, Whittaker and Ball 1997) that
sentencers are selective in commissioning PSRs. For example, where a long
custodial sentence is inevitable a PSR would normally be redundant.

The impact of plea on the length of sentence is considered below.

Cases committed for sentencing to the Crown Court

If a magistrates' court, having dealt with an adult offender for an offence
which is triable either-way, decides that the offence is so serious that it
requires a heavier sentence than they can impose, the case can be
committed to the Crown Court for sentencing. *Criminal Statistics England
and Wales* show that, in 1996, 4,600 defendants were committed for
sentence.

In this study 61 per cent of defendants committed for sentence were given a
custodial sentence. For those imprisoned, the average sentence length was
15.4 months but over a third (37 %) of those who were imprisoned received
a term that could have been imposed by magistrates. This means that overall
62 per cent of those committed for sentence received a penalty which could

have been imposed by magistrates. This is the same proportion as found in earlier research (Hedderman and Moxon, 1992).

Sentence discount following a guilty plea

Counsel should inform a client of the likelihood of a reduced sentence with a discount usually within the range of 25–33 per cent. The point at which the guilty plea was indicated to the court will be taken into account in deciding whether to give a reduced sentence. Last minute changes of plea are not looked upon so favourably[8] (Morton, 1994:27-9). The possibility of a reduced sentence is usually available even where the defendant does not have a realistic defence although, in R v Stabler,[9] the Appeal Court commented that 'we can see no ground for giving any discount in the circumstances of this particular case. This man had no alternative but to plead guilty'.

The Criminal Justice and Public Order Act 1994 (s48) formalised plea discounts. In considering whether to give a lighter sentence for a guilty plea, the court should take into account (i) the stage at which the intention to plead guilty was announced and (ii) the circumstances in which the intention to plead guilty was given.

Plea did not appear to influence the decision *whether* to impose a custodial sentence[10] but Figure 8.17 shows that it did affect the *length* of sentence, which was around a third less for those pleading guilty. Of course, the relationship between plea and sentence length is complex. The fact that the offender pleaded not guilty and was convicted after a trial closes off some forms of mitigation: it is difficult for the defence to argue that the offender is remorseful or has changed his or her lifestyle if the offence was not admitted. The difference in sentence length was greater than that found in previous studies: Moxon (1988:32) found that the average reduction where an offender pleaded guilty was 22 per cent. This may reflect the formalisation of discounts through the 1994 Act.

---

8   R v Hollington and Emmens (1986) 82 Cr App Rep 281.
9   R v Stabler (1984) 6 Cr App Rep (S) 129 (A).
10   Only in drug offences was there a statistically significant relationship between plea and the probability of receiving a custodial sentence: 84% of those who pleaded not guilty received a custodial sentence compared to 61% of

Figure 8.17: Average sentence length by plea, offenders receiving a custodial sentence only. (Source: Crown Court survey)

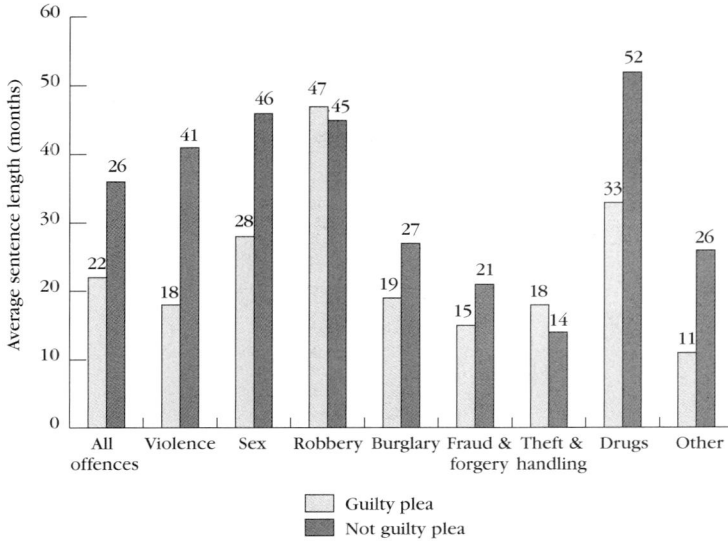

The impact of plea was particularly marked in violent and sexual offences because those charged with the most serious offences were more likely to have pleaded not guilty: for example, 70 per cent of those convicted of rape pleaded not guilty compared to 39 per cent of those who were convicted of another sexual offence. The average sentence length where an offender convicted of rape had pleaded not guilty was 8.1 years compared to 3.9 years where the offender had pleaded guilty. Of course, these large differences in sentence length may reflect very different types of offences within the category of rape.

Similarly 67 per cent of those convicted of assault causing grievous bodily harm with intent (s18) had pleaded guilty compared to 29 per cent of those sentenced for other crimes of violence. The average sentence where an offender was convicted of an assault (GBH s18) after pleading not guilty was four and a quarter years compared to three years where the offender had pleaded guilty, a difference of just over a third.

Timeliness of the guilty plea

Last minute guilty pleas attracted smaller discounts. Offenders who intimated that they would plead guilty from the outset were more likely to receive a shorter sentence than those who initially pleaded not guilty but changed their plea before trial; these in turn, received a shorter sentence than those who were convicted after a trial: 64 per cent who pleaded guilty from the outset received a sentence of less than 18 months compared to 55 per cent of those who had entered an initial plea of not guilty which they later changed. Of those who were found guilty after a trial, 45 per cent received a sentence of less than 18 months. The average length of sentence where the offender had pleaded guilty from the start was 21.8 months compared to 24.6 months where they had initially pleaded not guilty but eventually pleaded guilty and 36.4 months where the offender pleaded not guilty and was convicted after a trial.

The difference in length where the offender had entered an early guilty plea was relatively small but it does seem as if there has been a change in sentencers' decision-making in this area as previous studies found that those who changed their plea at the last minute received a bigger discount than those who pleaded guilty from the outset. For example, Moxon (1988:33) found that the average sentence length where the offender pleaded guilty from the outset was 21.1 months compared to 17.6 months where the offender changed his or her plea at the last minute. The change may reflect the reference to timeliness in the 1994 legislation, and perhaps also to the introduction of plea and direction hearings (PDHs) where issues such as the final charge are fixed prior to the trial date. This means that there are fewer cases where the offender pleads guilty to an altered charge on the day of trial.

Effect of the guilty plea on sentences other than custody

Where the offender was fined, those pleading guilty were fined less on average – £548, as against £835. There was no significant difference in the length of a CSO or probation order by plea.

Longer than normal sentences

The Criminal Justice Act 1991 introduced a new power to impose long sentences in violent and sexual offences where it was believed necessary to protect the public from serious harm from the offender (CJA 1991 S2(2)(b)). In this sample, just eight (3%) of offenders convicted of violent offences[11] and five (6%) of those convicted of sexual offences[12] were given a 'longer than normal' custodial sentence. For these few violence cases, the average length of a sentence passed under S2(2)b in a violent offence was 7.2 years compared to 2.3 where the sentence was not passed as a longer than normal term. In sexual offences, the averages were 5.1 years and 3.0 years respectively.

---

11 Of the eight violent offences, one was convicted of manslaughter, one attempted murder, four assault occasioning grievous bodily harm, one wounding and one of arson.

12 Of the five sexual offences which resulted in a longer than normal sentence one was of attempted rape and four of indecent assault.

Over the past few years, guidance from the Court of Appeal has accumulated on the circumstances where a longer than normal sentence is appropriate.[13]

All the sexual offenders who received a longer than normal sentence and the majority of violent offenders had a previous criminal record which included convictions for similar offences. In a typical example, the defendant pleaded guilty to manslaughter after he admitted strangling his partner. The judge accepted that the assault had been provoked and that he had not intended to kill his girlfriend. He had a number of previous convictions for assault and public order offences relating to his relationship with his ex-wife and at the time of this offence was subject to an injunction to keep away from his current girlfriend. Psychiatric reports stated that he had a personality disorder. Imposing a 12-year sentence, the judge said that the defendant's history of violence towards women with whom he had an intimate relationship made him a danger to any woman with whom he might form a close relationship in the future.

In a second case, the offender was convicted of indecent assault on his daughter, who was in her forties. He had a number of convictions for sexual offences and three years previously had received a custodial sentence for an assault on the same victim in which he had tied her up with metal chains and then applied an electric current to the chains so that she received serious burns. He received 10 years.

In five of the 13 cases the fact that the defendant was mentally ill was a factor in the decision to pass a longer than normal sentence. For example, in one case where the offender pleaded guilty to one charge of attempted rape, there was some discussion about whether the court should make a hospital order or whether a long prison sentence was more appropriate. This was a particularly unpleasant offence in which the defendant attempted to rape a 78-year-old women after he had broken into her house and found her asleep in bed. He had a number of previous convictions for sexual offences including one for burglary with intent to commit rape 10 years previously. Initially the judge considered making a hospital order, but psychiatric reports suggested that the defendant did not have a mental illness which would respond to treatment. The judge believed that the offender posed a serious risk to the public, and a discretionary life sentence was imposed.

Three first offenders in the sample were given a longer than normal sentence for serious offences. All were mentally ill and a closer study of the offences revealed a pattern of behaviour which posed a risk to public safety. In one example, the defendant was convicted of five charges of arson which had occurred on different days over a six-month period. This defendant received a five-year sentence.

---

13   These Court of Appeal judgments have been usefully reviewed by Henham (1996).

9 Suspended sentences in the Crown Court

Figure 9.1, shows that suspended sentences were most frequently given in fraud cases[1]. Previous research found that suspended sentences were often used where there had been breach of trust by the defendant (Moxon, 1988:34) and in the present sample such cases were three times as likely to result in a suspended sentence (6% compared with 2%).

Female defendants were more than four times as likely as male defendants to receive a suspended sentence: nine per cent of female defendants received a suspended sentence compared with only two per cent of males.

The average age of those given suspended sentences was 41 years, compared to 29 for those sentenced to immediate custody.

Figure 9.1: Proportionate use of suspended custody by offence group – offenders over 21 only (Source: Criminal Statistics 1996)

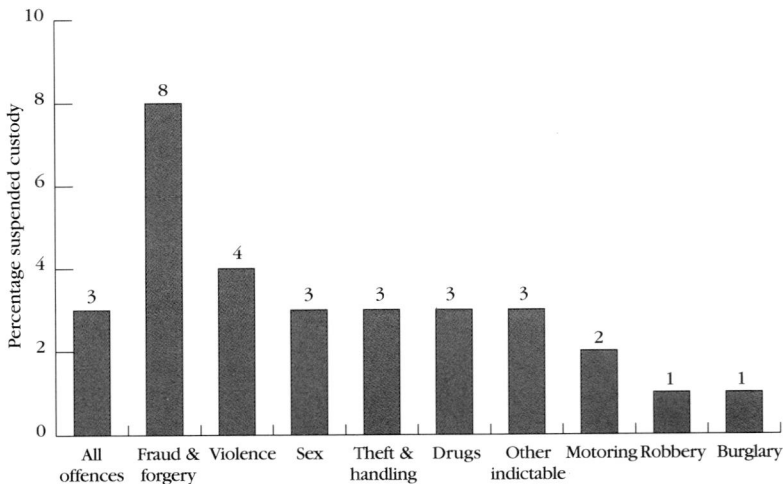

---

1   There has been a sharp fall in the use of suspended sentences for fraud and forgery from 11% in 1990 to 2% in 1995 (Criminal Statistics, 1995, Table 7C)

Reasons for suspending a custodial sentence

Table 9.1 shows the reasons that judges gave for suspending a custodial sentence. The most common reasons were that the defendant was ill, that they had to care for a dependent relative or that they were of previous good character. (Note that more than one reason could be given.)

Two-thirds of defendants where responsibility for dependent relatives was mentioned were female.

Table 9.1 Reasons for suspending a custodial sentence[1]

	No. of cases where factor mentioned	Percentage all cases receiving a suspended sentence
Physically/mentally ill	14	39
Looking after dependent relative	12	33
Previous good character	12	33
Personal difficulties/stress	2	6
Remorse/change in lifestyle	2	6

NOTE
1. Total number cases where reason was recorded 36
2. 'Other reasons' included 'being the victim of entrapment', that the defendant has given a great deal of help to the police', 'religious conversion' and 'under extreme stress at the time of the offence'.

Defendant's own illness or addiction

There were eight cases where the defendant's physical health was given as a reason for suspending sentence and in a further four cases the defendant's mental health had been a factor. In one example a 69-year-old man was convicted of two offences of assault causing grievous bodily harm and one lesser charge of assault causing actual bodily harm. The two victims (one of whom was his cohabitee) suffered cuts and bruises. He had previous convictions for similar offences, but the judge took into account the defendant's age and poor health.

In another case, a 28-year-old man, with one previous similar conviction, was convicted of two charges of handling and one of deception. The value of the goods was £150. However, another 40 offences were taken into consideration raising the sum to £1,932. Pre-sentence and psychiatric reports said that the defendant had 'severe mental health problems' requiring support. A suspended sentence and probation order was imposed.

Caring for dependent relatives

A third of suspended sentences involved cases where the defendants were caring for children or sick relatives. The majority of these (eight of the 12) involved women with child-care responsibilities. In one example a woman and her partner were convicted of handling stolen goods. They had a new baby, and while the father received a custodial sentence, the mother's sentence was suspended. In a second case, a husband and wife were both convicted of importing cocaine. The judge noted that the wife was less culpable than her husband and had no previous convictions. The judge said that a suspended sentence was justified because the wife was an asylum seeker whose young son's life would be in danger if he were to be deported to his country of origin while both his parents were in prison.

In another case a 35-year-old male received a suspended sentence following conviction on three drugs charges, which included supplying cannabis to his wife (who was addicted to opiates and suffering from hepatitis C). He said that he had given her cannabis in an attempt to wean her off more harmful drugs. He had no previous convictions. However, his wife was now missing from home and he was responsible for raising their three young children.

Parity of sentence

In two of the 36 cases, female co-defendants with children received a suspended sentence where their husband or cohabitee went to prison. However, there was one case where the judge said that the defendant deserved the same sentence as his co-defendant who had received a suspended sentence. In this case, a businessman with no previous convictions was convicted of fraud totalling £10,000. The offence arose out of problems he had with his business.

Previous good character

Earlier research (Moxon, 1988) found that the use of suspended sentences declined gradually as the number of previous convictions increased. In this present study, first offenders were twice as likely to receive a suspended sentence as offenders with a prior history of convictions (4% as against 2%). Numbers were too small to show whether this difference was due to chance, but the fact that this was often mentioned by judges suggests that lack of previous convictions carried weight.

10 Community sentences in the Crown Court

This chapter looks at the factors which led to some form of community sentence, and the factors associated with one type of community sentence rather than another.

Given the low use of fines and discharge, factors associated with community orders were the obverse of those linked with custody (Figure 10.1). Thus community sentences were used particularly heavily for younger offenders.

In this study, theft, fraud and public order offences were most likely to result in a community sentence, and sexual and robbery offences were least likely to attract such a sentence[1].

Figure 10.1: Factors associated with a community sentence (Source: Crown Court survey)

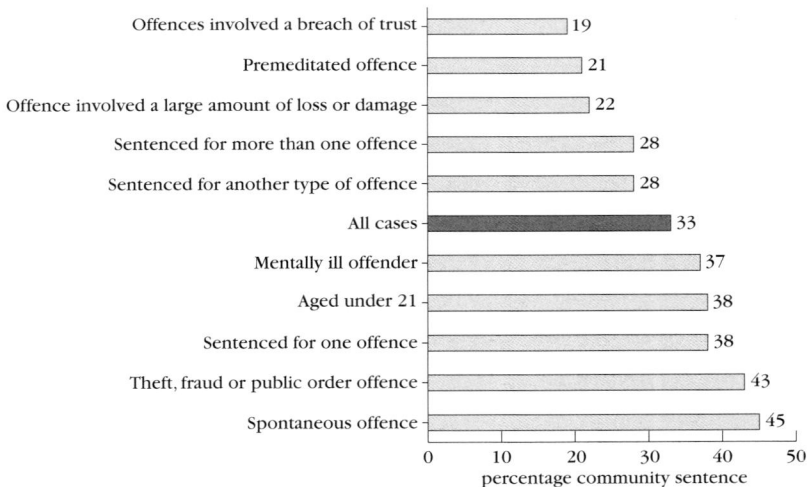

Factor	Percentage community sentence
Offences involved a breach of trust	19
Premeditated offence	21
Offence involved a large amount of loss or damage	22
Sentenced for more than one offence	28
Sentenced for another type of offence	28
All cases	33
Mentally ill offender	37
Aged under 21	38
Sentenced for one offence	38
Theft, fraud or public order offence	43
Spontaneous offence	45

---

1   It is difficult to make comparisons between offence categories because there were differences in the proportionate use of custody for each group and also in the characteristics of the cases within each category. A logistic regression model confirmed that a significantly higher proportion of theft and fraud offences resulted in a community sentence than would be expected on the basis of characteristics of the offence and the criminal history and personal characteristics of the offender. Conversely, sex offences, robbery and drugs were less likely to result in a community sentence.

Community sentences and the mentally ill

A fifth of the offenders were said to be suffering from some sort of mental illness or to be under *particular* stress. These offenders were less likely than others to receive a custodial sentence (Figure 10.2). This reflects a number of initiatives in recent years which have attempted to keep the mentally ill out of prison (for example, diversion from prosection schemes operate in some areas). A higher proportion of mentally ill than other offenders received a community sentence and, of those that did, most received probation or combination orders.

Figure 10.2: Sentencing patterns of the mentally ill (Source: Crown Court survey)

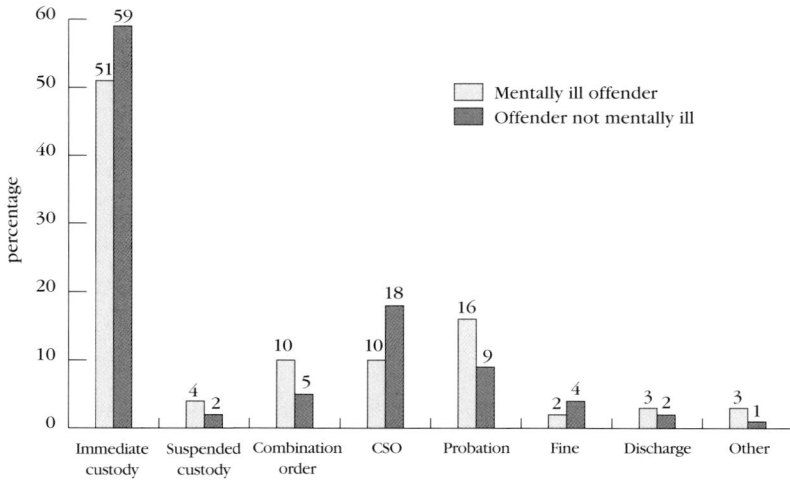

Women and community sentences

Figure 10.3 shows that women were more likely to receive a probation order than men: half of women who received a community sentence, received probation compared to just under a third of men. Barker (1993) concluded that this was partly because the types of manual work involved in CSO were not seen as suitable for women. Also CSO projects did not provide child care. The National Standards say that CSO schemes should be reviewed regularly to make sure that a wide range of placements are available.

Figure 10.3: Choice amongst community sentences by sex –
those sentenced to a community sentence only
(Source: Crown Court survey)

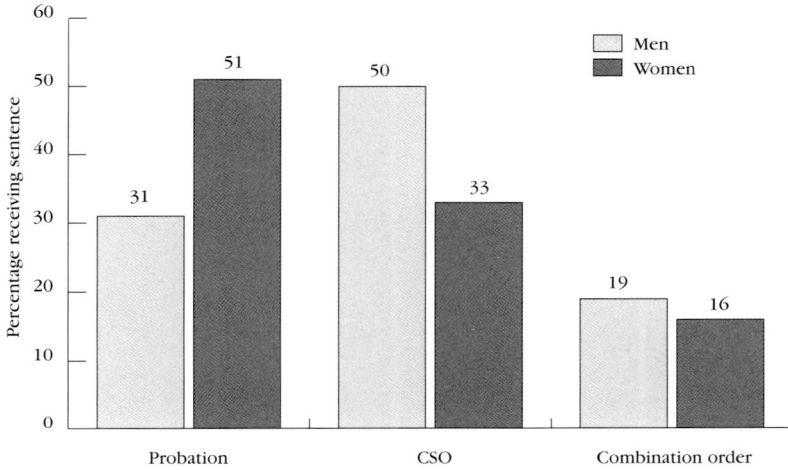

Probation orders

As compared with those given other community sentences, those given probation orders had more serious criminal records, were more likely to have a history of similar offences, and to have been subject to a court order at the time of the current offence. A higher proportion had been remanded in custody prior to sentencing.

Over a third of those who received a probation order were either mentally ill or under stress (Table 10.1). Almost a fifth were addicted to alcohol or drugs.

Table 10.1 Characteristics of those receiving combination orders, community service orders and probation orders
(Crown Court survey)

	% Probation order	% community service order	% combination order
Offence-related factors			
Premeditated offence	14	14	28
More than one offence	47	31	56
Offender-related factors			
Addicted to drugs/alcohol	17	3	14
Employed	17	51	32
Previous convictions	77	58	67
Similar convictions	43	38	19
Changes in lifestyle since the offence	13	8	12
Mentally ill/stressed	35	16	38
Subject to a court order at time of offence	32	12	27
Other factors			
Remanded in custody prior to sentence	29	3	14

Note:
1. As a proportion of all offenders sentenced to a community sentence with previous convictions

Community sentences were rarely used for sex offenders. Five of the six sex offenders who received a community sentence were given probation orders. Three were required to attend special sex offenders groups organised by the probation service.

Community service orders (CSOs)

Table 10.1 shows that CSOs were used for first offenders much more often than probation or combination orders. Those receiving community service tended to be older than those sentenced to probation or a combination order and they were more likely to have settled lifestyles: only three per cent had problems with alcohol or drugs and only 16 per cent were mentally ill or stressed. This is not surprising as community service on its own is generally seen as unsuitable for people with an unsettled lifestyle who would be highly likely to breach the order (Ellis, Hedderman and Mortimer, 1996).

Combination orders

Drugs offences apart, there was no particular pattern to the offence types that attracted combination orders. As seen in Chapter 4, combination orders were used for more serious offenders than CSO or probation alone in the magistrates' courts. In the Crown Court, the proportion of offenders with previous convictions, and convictions for similar offences, was less than the proportion for offenders on probation. However, the cases which resulted in combination orders were more likely to have been premeditated and to have involved more than one offence.

Offenders who were given combination orders had some elements in common with those given probation. In particular, similar numbers were suffering from mental illness or stress, or had problems with alcohol or drugs.[2] Other studies have found that there is a high level of breach associated with combination orders where the probation officer had said in the PSR that they were not suitable for CSO and it is possible that these orders are being given to some people who will find it difficult to comply with the CSO elements of the order (Ellis, Hedderman and Mortimer, 1996).

Additional requirements

Table 10.2 shows that over a fifth of additional requirements were for 'intensive probation'. This can include a range of activities but generally means that the offender has much more contact with the probation officer, often seeing him or her once or twice a week. The possibility of making offenders receive treatment for a drugs or alcohol dependency as a requirement of probation was introduced by the CJA in 1991. A fifth of additional requirements were to receive treatment for drug dependency and a further seven per cent involved receiving treatment for alcohol dependency. It is possible that many of the other offenders who received probation would have attended organised group activities voluntarily: a recent survey of people on probation found that 40 per cent had attended some type of group activity either as an additional requirement of probation ordered by the court or voluntarily at the suggestion of the probation officer. The activities most frequently attended were groups dealing with alcohol problems, a day centre or employment or training scheme (Mair and May, 1997).

---

2   This finding was confirmed by a discriminant analysis which used variables identified in Table 10.2 as associated with the choice between community orders, to create a model predicting the cases which would get different community orders. The model was good at correctly predicting those who received a CSO, it was less good at predicting who would receive a probation order or a combination order because these were less clearly differentiated. This analysis is shown in Table D.15, Appendix D.

Table 10.2 Additional requirements to probation orders (Crown Court survey)

	Number	% cases where additional requirements were made
Intensive probation	21	28
Treatment or counselling for a drug-related problem	16	22
Alcohol related treatment or counselling	5	7
Psychiatric or other medical treatment	11	15
Residence at a hostel	8	11
Persistent offender programme	5	7
Sex offender programme	3	4
Motor-project	3	4
Anger-management	3	4
Women offender group	1	1
Employment programme	1	1
'Cognitive thinking' group	1	1
Total number of cases where information available		74

Note 1. More than one additional requirement could be made to each order

11 Fines and compensation orders in the Crown Court

Although financial penalties are used extensively in magistrates' courts, they are used predominantly for minor offences and are little used by the Crown Court. Only six per cent of defendants sentenced in the Crown Court were fined and in our sample only three per cent were fined. Both employment status and previous convictions were strongly associated with use of fines. *Criminal Statistics* show that, at the Crown Court, the fine is used predominantly for theft, drugs and public order offences, and that motoring offences attract the largest proportion of fines (Figure 11.1). Ten per cent of employed first offenders were fined compared to just two per cent of unemployed first offenders. Among those with previous convictions, eight per cent of unemployed offenders were fined but none of the unemployed were fined. (Unemployed offenders were more likely to receive a community sentence, particularly probation or a combination order (Table D19, Appendix D).

Figure 11.1: Proportionate use of the fine by offences – Crown Court (Source: Criminal Statistics 1996)

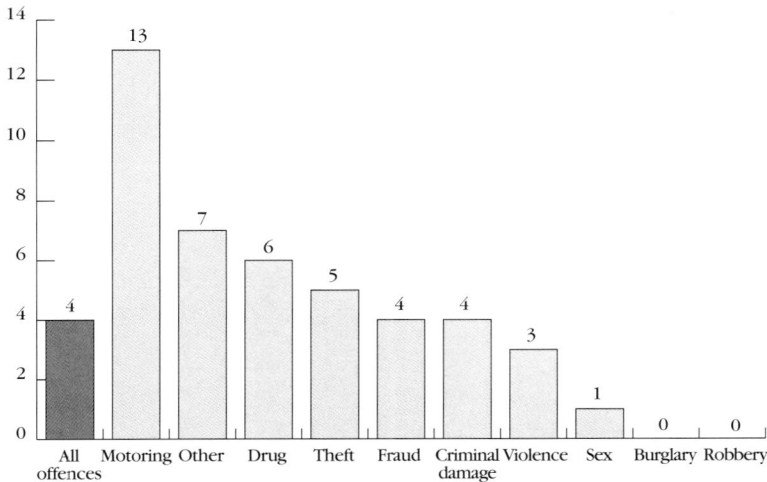

Men were more likely to be fined than women: *Criminal Statistics* shows that in 1995 five per cent of men and three per cent of women sentenced at the Crown Court were fined.[1] Dowds and Hedderman (1997) found that men convicted of violent offences were twice as likely as women convicted of the same offence to be fined.

Fixing the size of a fine

There is no limit to the size of the fine the Crown Court can impose.[2] Fifty-eight per cent were fined less than £250, though the average was £620 as this figure was skewed by a small number of very large fines.

Fining unemployed people

As at magistrates' courts, people in work were given larger fines than unemployed offenders reflecting the requirement for courts to take the means of the offender into account in setting fines. Men had higher average fines than women regardless of their employment status (Figure 11.2).

The average fine for an unemployed man was £340 which would take one year and four months to pay at the rate of £5 a week, generally regarded as the upper limit that someone on state benefits can afford. It would take two and half years to pay an average fne through deductions from income support. Just under a fifth (18%) of unemployed men were fined more than £500. These offenders would take at least four years to pay the fine at current rates unless they had savings.

The Court of Appeal has expressed concern about the ability of people on low incomes to pay fines over a long period of time.[3] L.J. Staughton said:

> *What troubles me about these cases is the size of fines which those on income support were expected to pay out of resources which are only sufficient for the necessities of life. Over a short period of time the money provided as income support may be sufficient for paying small, but regular, amounts towards fines. But, as everyone knows, there are contingencies which occur and will strain a tight budget.*

It was recommended that fines for people on low incomes should be capable of being paid in a matter of weeks and regular payments enforced.

---

1   A similar pattern was found in magistrates' courts.
2   In Ronson ((1981) Crim L R 794) the Court of Appeal upheld a fine of £5 million as well as a term of imprisonment.
3   R v Stockport Justices ex parte Peter Conlon and R v Newark Justices ex parte Kennaghan.

Figure 11.2: Average fine by employment status and sex (Source: Crown Court survey)

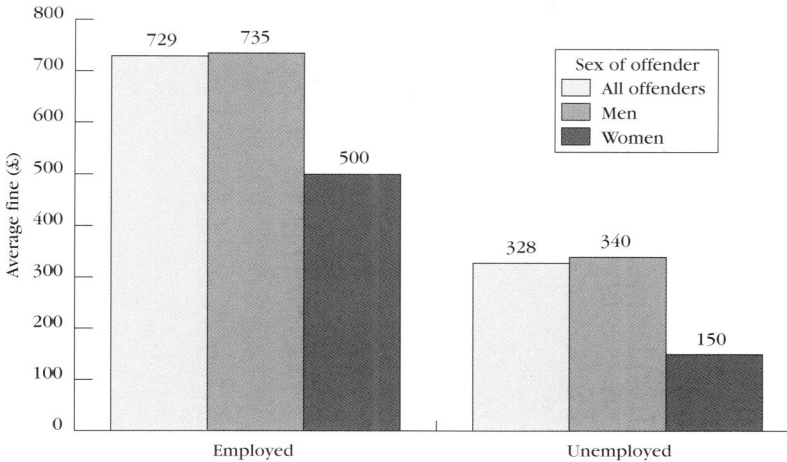

Compensation

By 1996, only eight per cent of all offenders sentenced at the Crown Court were ordered to pay some form of compensation (Figure 11.3). There has been a similar trend in magistrates' courts in England and Wales and in Scotland (Hamilton and Wisniewski, 1996:11). A partial explanation of this fall in the use of compensation at the Crown Court is the increase in the use of custody, as compensation is rarely practicable where the offender goes to prison. However, this cannot wholly explain the reduction as in 1995, 17 per cent of offenders who received a non-custodial sentence at the Crown Court were ordered to pay compensation compared to 22 per cent in 1990.

Figure 11.3: Proportion of cases in which offender ordered to pay compensation – Crown Court only (Source: Crown Court survey)

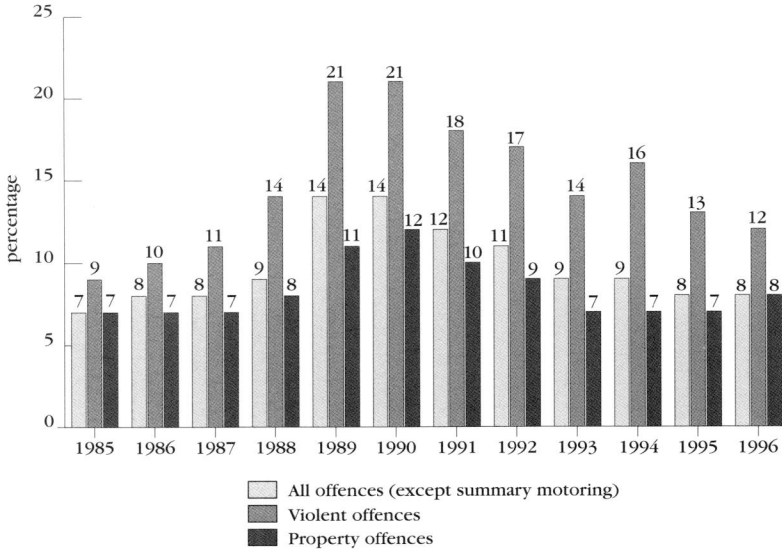

In 1996, only 126 offenders were ordered to pay compensation as their sole sentence by the Crown Court. There was just one case in the present sample where compensation was the only sentence. The offender, a 23-year-old man with mental health problems, was convicted of two offences of assault (causing grievous bodily harm (s20)). The victims of the attack were both young men who had no relationship to the offender. He was already serving a custodial sentence for another assault charge and was ordered to pay £150 in compensation. The judge said that, if he had not been in prison, this sentence would have been too lenient. However, in the circumstances, the judge believed that extending the period of time spent in custody would not serve any purpose.

The use of compensation orders in a wide variety of offences is examined below, paying particular attention to the reasons that judges gave for not awarding compensation in order to identify measures that would encourage them to use it more frequently.

The use of compensation orders

Compensation was most frequently awarded for violent, 'other' and sex offences (Figure 11.4). Property offences (burglary, theft and deception) were much less likely to result in compensation. The average amount of compensation awarded was £280, although in fraud and forgery cases the average award was much higher (£625).

Figure 11.4: Proportionate use of compensation by offence type. Cases resulting in a non-custodial sentence only (Source: Crown Court survey)

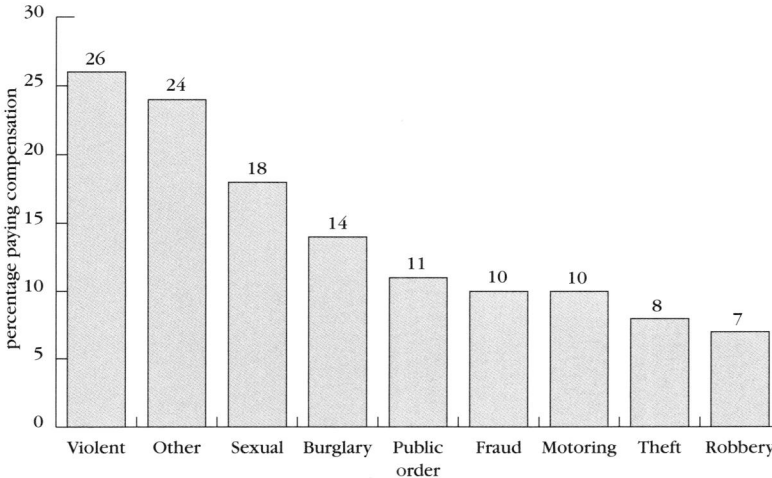

Compensation for personal injury

In violent offences, compensation was most likely to be awarded in cases where the victim was acquainted with the offender rather than where the offence arose out of a 'domestic' situation or where there was no relationship between the victim and offender (Table 11.3).

Table 11.3 Compensation by relationship to the offender in violent offences (Source: Crown Court survey)

	Number	% cases where compensation awarded
Partner/family member	15	20
Friend or acquaintance	24	42
Stranger	48	29
Police officer/other in position of authority[2]	7	30

Notes:
1. Custodial sentences were excluded because compensation was rarely awarded. Information was missing for 21 cases.
2. Includes store detectives, paramedics etc.

The recommended compensation for a bruise is currently £75, for a facial scar which leaves the victim permanently disfigured £750 and for a broken arm £2,500. In this study, the average amount awarded for a minor injury (cut or a bruise) was £254 while, for a more serious injury, the average award was £572. Interestingly, where the victim had not been physically hurt in the offence and so compensation was for the distress or inconvenience suffered as a result of the offence, the average award was £398.

Combining compensation and other sentences

The CJA 1991 requires a court to consider whether a fine or compensation order should be imposed alongside a suspended sentence. In this study, almost ten per cent of those who were given a suspended custodial sentence were also required to pay a compensation order. Over a fifth of those fined were ordered to pay compensation as well (Figure 11.5).

Figure 11.5: Proportionate use of compensation by main sentence (Source: Crown Court survey)

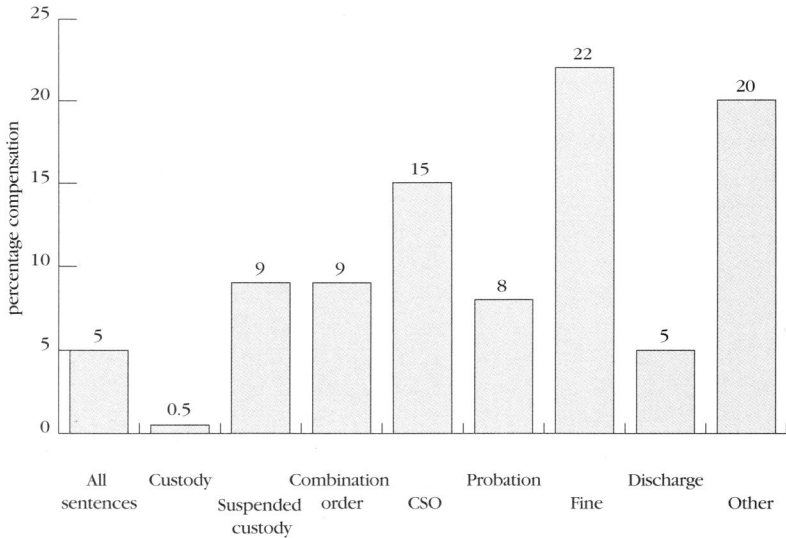

Reasons for not awarding compensation

Observers were asked to record the reasons given for not awarding compensation. Figure 11.6 shows that in the majority of cases nothing was said in court which would explain why compensation was not awarded. Often the reason will have been obvious - for example, beause a prison sentence was imposed, or because the property was recovered.

Figure 11.6: Reasons for not awarding compensation given by judges. Excluding cases which received a custodial sentence (Source: Crown Court survey)

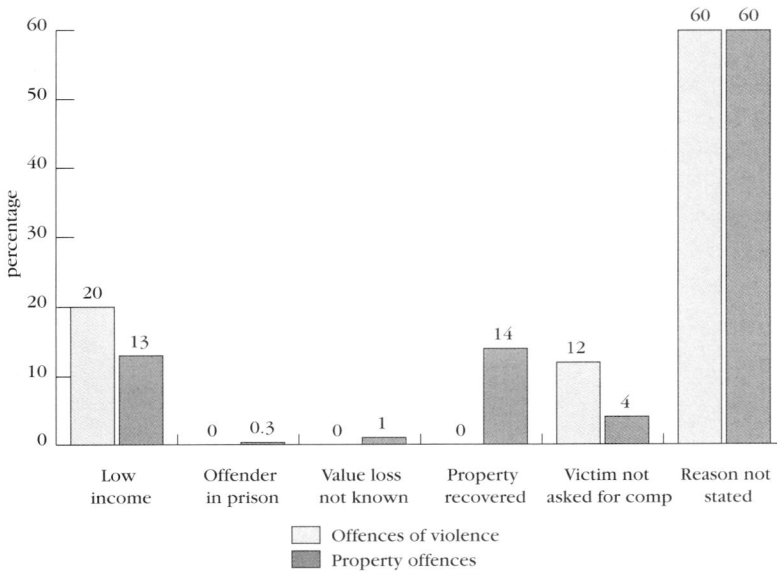

The main reason that judges gave for not awarding compensation in violent offences and in 13 per cent of property offences was that the offender could not afford to pay. Offenders in work were twice as likely to have a compensation order made against them as those who were unemployed. Of those offenders in work convicted of a violent or property offence and who received a non-custodial sentence, 22 per cent had a compensation order made against them compared to 10 per cent of unemployed offenders.

In 12 per cent of violent and four per cent of property offences, the reason given for not awarding compensation was that it had not been requested by the victim. The Court of Appeal[4] has cautioned sentencers against 'simply plucking a figure out of the air' and the amount of compensation should either be agreed between the parties or established by evidence. This emphasises the need for the prosecutor to address the issue of compensaton during the sentence hearing.

---

4   Swan (1984) 6 Cr App R (S) 22 per Kilner Brown J.

Part 4

Extra-legal factors in sentencing and discussion

Claire Flood-Page

12 Sentencing of ethnic minority offenders, men and women and young offenders

Comparisons of sentences for different groups were not a central feature of the study, and the numbers of ethnic minorities and of women in the sample were relatively small. However, past research has pointed to some differences in the sentencing of different ethnic groups, as well as differences in sentencing of males and females. We therefore looked at such evidence as we had.

Race and sentencing

Previous research has shown that ethnic minorities are treated and act in different ways at the key stages in criminal process. For example, there is a lot of evidence that Afro-Caribbeans are less likely to admit an offence and therefore make themselves ineligible for a caution (FitzGerald, 1993; Commission for Racial Equality, 1992). This also means that they are less likely to benefit from the discount for a guilty plea.

For those found guilty, there has been considerable discussion of whether the apparent differences in sentencing are due to ethnic or other factors. This was reviewed by FitzGerald (1993) in a report prepared for the Royal Commission on Criminal Justice. The largest studies have consistently found a higher rate of custodial sentences for Afro-Caribbean offenders, although for Asians several studies have suggested that the custody rates might be lower than for whites (*Statistical Bulletin* 6/89; Walker, 1988, 1989). In the largest Crown Court study of race and sentencing, Hood (1992) found some evidence of discrimination, though this was confined to just one of the four Crown Court centres in the study.

In any future research focusing specifically on ethnic minorities, it needs to be borne in mind that the fairly crude ethnic breakdowns used in most studies (including this one) simplify a complex picture. Among the 'Asian' group are a number of ethnic minorities who differ in their socio-economic position (e.g., Pakistanis and Bangladeshis suffer higher rates of unemployment than Indians or East African Asians) and there is some evidence that, while the proportions of Indians and Bangladeshis in prison is the same as in the general population, there are a disproportionately high number of Pakistanis in prison (Home Office, 1992:11). There are also important differences between black people of Caribbean origin (most of whom are British citizens) and Africans (some of whom are temporarily in the UK). A full assessment of ethnic differences would require a study to distinguish not only between whites and ethnic minorities, but also between different groups within the broad ethnic categories (FitzGerald, 1993:39).

Magistrates' courts

Of the magistrates' court sample, 18 per cent were non-white (286 male and 49 female black offenders and 192 male and 49 female Asian offenders). The small number of female offenders in ethnic minority samples meant that the analysis was confined to males.

Figure 12.1: Sentencing of male ethnic minority offenders (Source: Magistrates' courts survey)

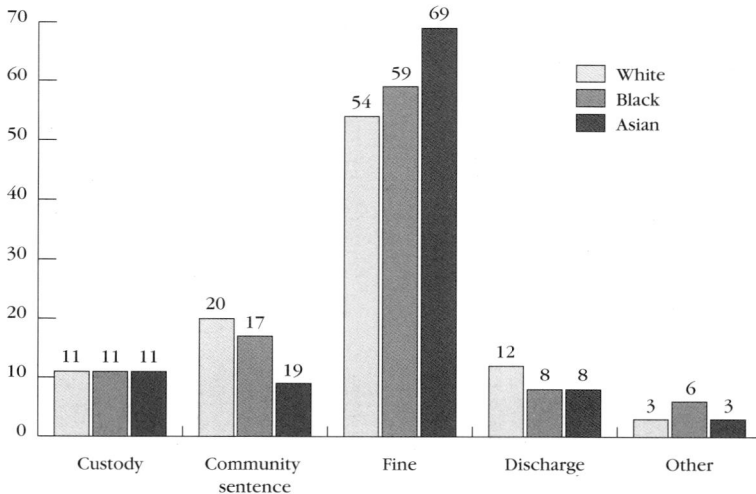

Figure 12.1 shows that the differences in the sentencing of ethnic minorities were complex. The same proportion of white, black and Asian men received

a custodial sentence. Slightly more white and black offenders received a community sentence. A higher proportion of Asian men were fined. Much of these differences can be explained by the characteristics of offenders from different ethnic groups (Table 12.1).

Ninety-two per cent of white defendants in this sample pleaded guilty compared to 85 per cent of black and 86 per cent of Asian defendants. Ethnic minorities are less likely to have a pre-sentence report which makes a community sentence less likely. This, in turn, is linked to the fact that a PSR is not normally prepared in advance for those pleading not guilty.

Table 12.1 Differences between male offenders by ethnic group (Source: Magistrates' courts survey)

	White %	Black %	Asian %
Offence type			
Violence	5	5	3
Sex	0.2	0.7	0.5
Burglary	4	2	1
Theft	18	14	9
Fraud / handling	2	4	2
Drugs	6	11	4
Criminal damage	6	5	1
Other indictable	2	4	2
Summary non-monitoring	17	14	14
Summary motoring	40	41	65
First offender	30	27	44
Sentenced with a pre-sentence report	35	29	24
Pleaded guilty	92	85	86
Subject to an earlier court order			
No previous orders	74	77	90
In breach of bail	8	12	4
Subject to order other than bail	18	12	6
Remanded in custody	14	11	10
Unemployed	64	75	48
Total number	1963	286	192

Note:
1. Because there were few ethnic minority women in the sample, this analysis focuses on men.

There were also differences between ethnic groups in the types of offences: two-thirds of Asian men were sentenced for motoring offences compared to around two-fifths of white and black men. A higher proportion of black men were sentenced for drug offences.

In further analysis (see Table C9 Appendix C) the similarity in custody for blacks and whites remained after allowing for other factors. Asian men were significantly more likely to be sentenced to custody than would have been expected on the basis of their offence and other factors. However, variables such as the type and number of offences, their plea, whether they were subject to a court order when they committed the offence, being mentally ill or whether the offence was premeditated explained more of the variation in custody rates than ethnic origin.

Crown Court

Of the Crown Court sample, 22 per cent were non-white (267 male and 46 female black offenders and 70 male and six female Asian offenders).

Table 12.2 shows that three-quarters of white defendants in this sample pleaded guilty compared to two-thirds of black and Asian defendants. White and black defendants were more likely than Asians to have a pre-sentence report, which tends to preclude a community sentence.

There are also differences in the type of offences for which offenders from different ethnic groups are sentenced. Hood (1992:196) found that black offenders sentenced in the Crown Court were more likely than white or Asian offenders to have been convicted of robbery or supplying drugs and fewer were dealt with for burglary, theft or fraud. In the present study a higher proportion of black defendants were sentenced for drug offences and robbery; rather fewer were sentenced for violence. A high proportion of Asian offenders (26%) were convicted of violent offences but were much less likely to be sentenced for burglary or robbery than either white or black offenders.

Published statistics consistently show greater over-representation of Afro-Caribbeans in the remand population than among sentenced prisoners. In this sample black offenders were more likely to have been remanded in custody than white defendants. A number of factors mean that black defendants are more likely to be tried in the Crown Court than white defendants: they are more likely to be charged with indictable-only offences (especially robbery) and a higher proportion of black defendants charged with a triable-either-way offence were committed for trial at the Crown Court – often because they chose jury trial.

Table 12.2 Differences between male offenders by ethnic group and type of offence (Crown Court survey)

	White %	Black %	Asian %
Offence type			
Violence	17	13	26
Sex	5	3	6
Robbery	6	9	1
Burglary	18	17	9
Theft	16	19	17
Fraud or deception	9	10	13
Drugs	14	20	9
Public order	6	5	9
Motoring	5	3	4
Other indictable	4	2	7
Offender details			
First offender	27	30	50
Sentenced with a PSR	88	87	79
Pleaded guilty	75	66	65
Breach of a court order	28	27	16
Remanded in custody	37	42	20
Unemployed	65	77	64
Total number	1173	267	70

Note:1. All factors shown were significant at the 5% level. Women were excluded from the analysis because of the small numbers of ethnic minority women in the sample.

Figure 12.2 shows that, among first offenders, a similar proportion of white, black and Asian men received a custodial sentence. A slightly higher proportion of black offenders received a community sentence, although this was not statistically significant at the five per cent level. Among those with previous convictions, although a higher proportion of Asians than whites or blacks received a custodial sentence, the difference was not statistically significant (Figure 12.3).

Figure 12.2: Sentencing of male first offenders by ethnic appearance
(Source: Crown Court survey)

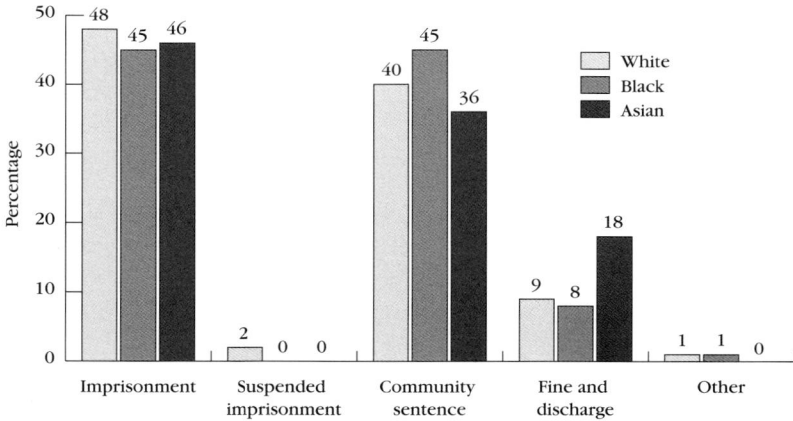

Figure 12.3: Sentencing of male offenders with previous convictions by ethnic origin
(Source: Crown Court survey)

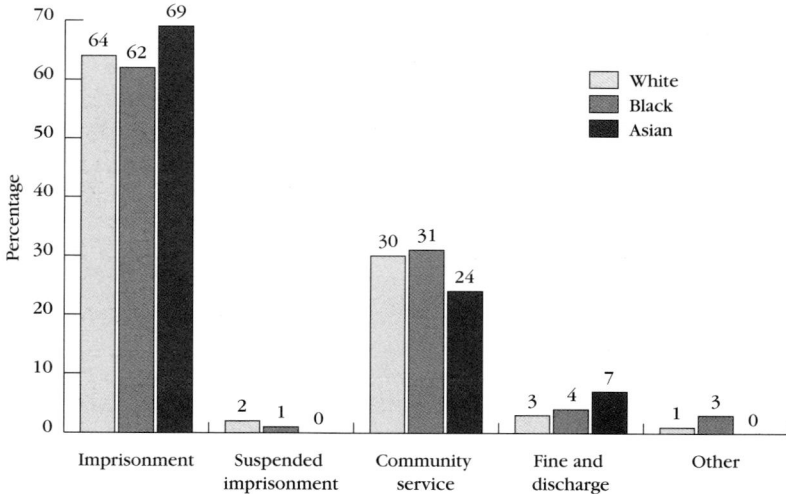

That ethnic minority males were not significantly more likely to receive a custodial sentence than white males when other factors were taken into account was confirmed by further analysis. The differences in custody rates were explained by variables such as the type and number of offences, their plea, whether they were subject to a court order when they committed the offence, being mentally ill or whether the offence was spontaneous.

Sentencing of men and women

The effect which the sex of the offender has on sentencing has been the subject of a recent major Home Office study (Hedderman and Gelsthorpe, 1997). That study found that, overall, women received more lenient treatment than men, although the picture was not straightforward. For example, courts were more reluctant to fine women, and although this meant that more received discharges, it also meant that they were more likely to move up the scale to a community sentence.

There are marked differences in the pattern of offending and among indictable offences, theft forms a larger proportion of offences committed by women (66% of offences) than by men (44% of offences); for burglary and drug offences the situation is reversed.

Even allowing for their much lower rate of offending, females are much less likely to be prosecuted: in 1995, 59 per cent of women convicted or cautioned for indictable offences were cautioned, compared to 37 per cent of men. Women are less likely to be remanded in custody than men, reflecting the fact that they were less likely to have previously breached bail or to have been charged with a further offence while on bail or be of no fixed abode (Morgan and Pearce, 1989).

Criminal Statistics, England and Wales, 1995 showed that twice as many men (9.5%) as women (4.6%) sentenced for an indictable offence received a custodial sentence. Men were also more likely to be fined than women, with a higher proportion of women receiving a conditional discharge. Just under 30 per cent of both men and women received a community penalty. There is a difference in the choice between community sentences, however, with more women receiving probation and more men being given CSOs.

Figure 12.4: Sentencing of of men and women first offenders in Magistrates's courts (Source: Magistrates' courts survey)

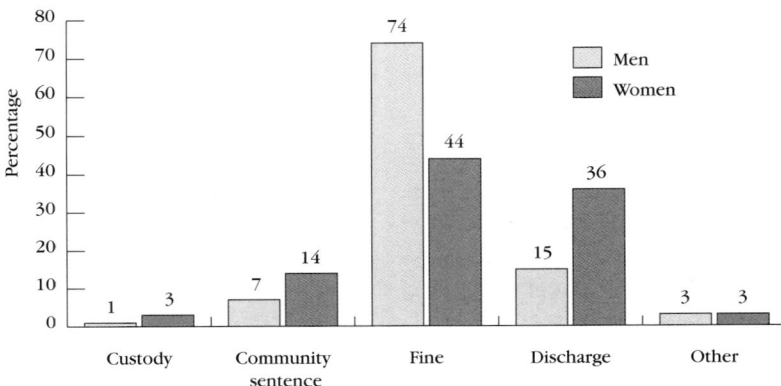

Figure 12.5: Sentencing of men and women first offenders in the Crown Court
(Source: Crown Court survey)

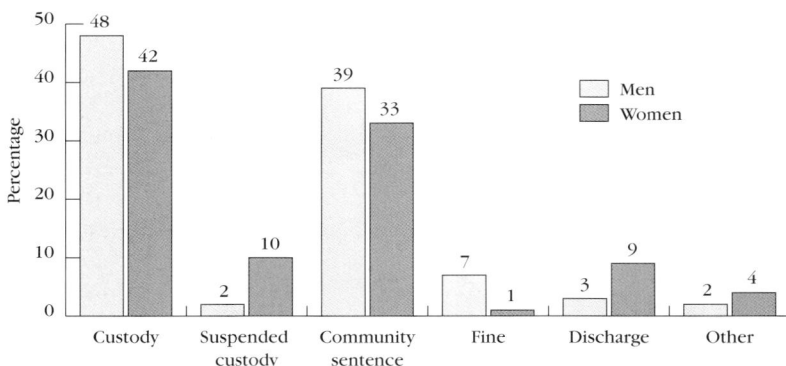

In this study (Figures 12.4 and 12.5) a higher proportion of male first offenders received a custodial sentence than female first offenders in the Crown Court. So few first offenders received custodial sentences in magistrates courts sample that the difference was not significant. Men with previous convictions were four times as likely to receive a custodial sentence than women who were repeat offenders in magistrates' courts (Figure 12.6). In the Crown Court male repeat offenders were one-and-a-half times as likely to receive a custodial sentence as women.

Further analysis confirmed that men had a significantly higher probability of receiving a custodial sentence than women even when other factors were taken into account. (Table C12, Appendix C)

Figure 12.6: Comparison of sentencing of men and women with previous convictions in Magistrates' court
(Source: Magistrates' courts survey)

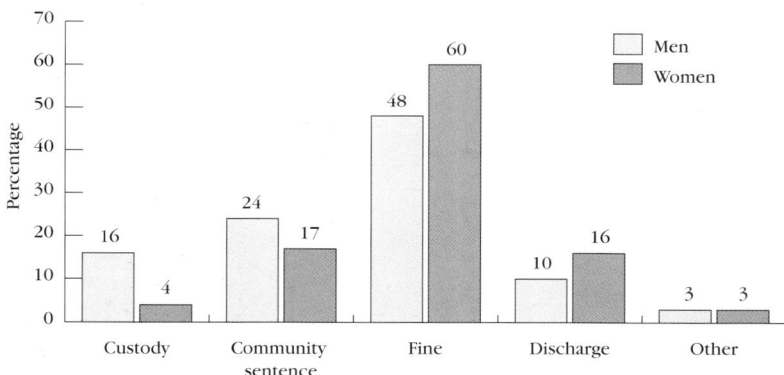

Figure 12.7: Sentencing of men and women with previous convictions (Source: Crown Court survey)

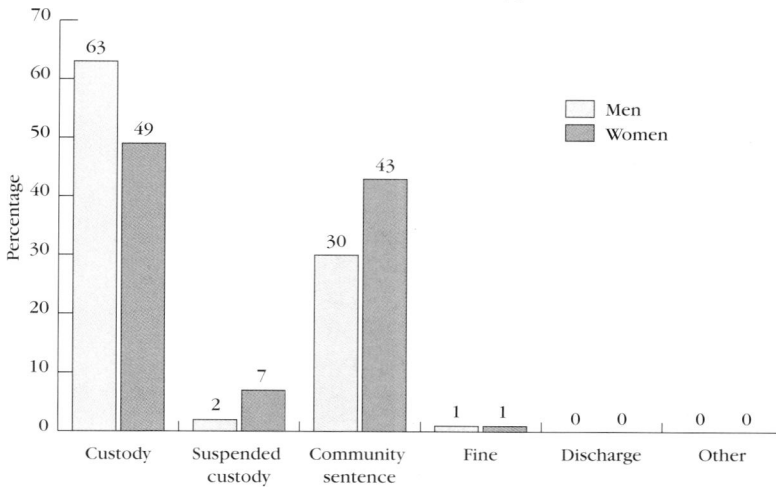

Young offenders in the Crown Court

The study did not cover the Youth Court, which is the forum in which magistrates deal with most young offenders. More serious cases go to the Crown Court, and the following description is confined to these.

Only four per cent of the sample were aged 17 or under, of whom half were aged 17. In this small group, one-third was sentenced for robbery compared to just five per cent of defendants aged 18 and over. Of offenders under 18, 53 per cent received a custodial sentence compared to 58 per cent of older offenders. A more telling comparison is that offenders aged 17 or under were much less likely to receive a custodial sentence for robbery: half of offenders in the younger age group received a custodial sentence for robbery compared to 86 per cent of offenders aged 18 or over. In the most serious case involving juveniles in the sample, a 15-year-old boy and a girl aged 14 were charged with manslaughter and robbery. They had robbed an 83-year-old woman who fell downstairs during the incident, fracturing her skull and dislocating her shoulder. She later died as a result of complications. The boy had one previous conviction for burglary; the girl had no previous convictions. The pre-sentence reports described the difficult home lives of the two defendants. The boy received a sentence of five years' detention while the girl received a two year supervision order. The girl was only 13 at the time of the offence which meant she was not eligible for a detention order. The judge said that these sentences did not reflect the seriousness of the crime, but his powers were limited by statute.

There were several cases where young offenders were sentenced with older co-defendants. In such cases the younger person often played a minor role, very much under the influence of the older person. In one case a 16-year-old was convicted with his older (34-year-old) brother of attempted robbery. The younger defendant was 14 at the time of the offence, and was of limited intelligence. They had threatened a prostitute with a knife and tried to rob her. Neither defendant had previous convictions. The older brother received a two-year prison sentence while the 16-year-old received an attendance order for 20 hours.

In another case a 15-year-old boy with one previous conviction for theft was sentenced for conspiracy to supply Class A drugs. He was described as a homeless, vulnerable youth who was approached by a much older man to act as a 'runner', supplying drugs in repayment for £80 a day. He received a two year supervision order, although the judge felt that the offence justified a custodial sentence, which would have been imposed but for the boy's vulnerability.

Figure 12.8 shows that a greater proportion of those aged 17 and under received a community sentence. The actual options for community sentences are different for the younger age group, with those aged under 16 not eligible for community service or combination orders, but a supervision order may be imposed. Of those aged 16 or 17, 27 per cent received a probation order compared to 11 per cent of offenders aged 18 or over.

Figure 12.8: Sentencing of all offenders by age in the court (Source: Crown Court survey)

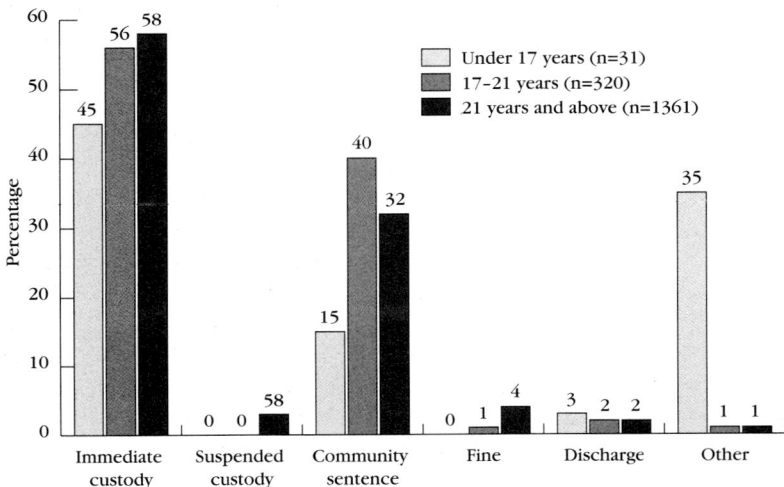

13 Where next?

Past research has shown considerable differences in the sentencing tariffs applied by magistrates' courts and the Crown Court respectively, but the present study shows that case factors do pull in the same direction for both magistrates and judges. However, as the discussion of recent sentencing trends in Chapter 2 indicated, the weight given to case factors changes over time: since 1993 it is sentencing practice, not the legal framework, that has changed. A particular feature has been the switch from community penalties to immediate custody, encouraged by the fact that the option of suspending a custodial sentence has been largely closed off.

Custody

Consideration of when custody *should* be used is outside the scope of this study. In presenting detailed information about the factors which lead sentencers to conclude that the custody threshold has been reached, the aim has been to inform future debate. In terms of crime control, imprisonment offers obvious benefits through incapacitation, though in terms of reconvictions there is remarkably little to choose between sentences. Some recent research, however, suggests that there are crime-reduction strategies which can cut crime by more than imprisonment for each pound spent (see Ekblom, Law and Sutton, 1996, for an analysis of the cost-effectiveness of safer cities programmes in reducing burglary).

There has been a sharp fall in suspended sentences in recent years, so that they are hardly used at all by magistrates, and their use has fallen by around four-fifths at the Crown Court. As Chapter 2 shows, there was a two-stage switch, first from suspended sentences to community sentences, and then from community sentences to immediate custody. Although the process is quite a complex one, it seems highly likely that some cases which a few years ago would have attracted a suspended sentence have, by stages, moved to immediate custody. This is because the thrust of the 1991 Act was away from custody, which meant that the constraints on suspended sentences could be imposed without risking a major shift to immediate custody; but the constraints remained when the use of custody began to rise in 1992.

Community sentences

Differing views emerged among magistrates about community sentences:

- some magistrates saw probation as a soft option, while others felt it was potentially demanding for those with very disorganised lifestyles; it called for a measure of self-discipline, and required offending behaviour to be challenged in a way which prison usually did not

- there was a lack of consensus as to whether there was a tariff among community sentences, or whether it was a matter of selecting the sentence simply according to the needs of the offender

- some magistrates felt that the types of activities available at attendance centres did not amount to punishment

- the variation between areas in their use of additional requirements bore out the finding of previous research that some probation areas had a policy of never recommending them in PSRs (Home Office, 1996).

These conflicting views suggest that in some cases there was scope both for improving the content of orders and for demonstrating their value to magistrates. Improving sentencers' confidence in such orders could also help boost public confidence in them. Although overall reconviction rates for differed penalties do not vary much after allowing for key factors (see, for example, Lloyd, Mair and Hough; 1995, Whittaker, 1997), there is some evidence that certain programmes (prison or probation) can help some offenders – eg programmes to tackle drug addiction. Future research will evaluate some of the individual probation programmes, which should help to identify the most successful strategies. This should help in developing good practice, and thereby building judicial and public confidence. It cannot be emphasised too strongly that magistrates (and no doubt judges too) are influenced by evidence of success in diverting offenders from crime when deciding what sort of sentence to impose, where the seriousness of the case does not make custody the only realistic choice.

Fines

Where custody is not needed in order to protect the public or to punish adequately, fines are a legitimate consideration. It is not altogether clear why fines have fallen into such disfavour over the past 20 years, but the increase in unemployment, the proliferation of other sentencing options and the spread of cautioning (which diverts minor cases) have no doubt played a part. But given that fines yield revenue and are associated with reconviction rates no higher (and if anything slightly lower) than other sentences, there is a strong case for their revival. Put another way, courts used to impose fines in many instances where they would not use them now. There is no evidence that the move away from fines has yielded any benefits in terms of crime reduction. It is of interest that the introduction of unit fines was accompanied by increased use of fines, which was reversed when they were abolished. The Magistrates' Association's recent advocacy of a more structured approach to relating fines to means could be helpful in halting the decline in the use of fines (which is still continuing).

Compensation

There seems to have been a general disenchantment with financial penalties, with compensation orders dropping along with fines. The requirement to give reasons for not awarding compensation seems to be widely ignored, even though it is reiterated throughout the Magistrates' Association guidelines. Often the reasons will be both sound and obvious, but not always. More worryingly, it was still quite common for compensation to be reduced for lack of means where the offender was nevertheless fined or ordered to pay costs. It seems that the need to give precedence to compensation where the offender's means will not run to both full compensation and a fine is often overlooked.

Consistency

The discussion so far has focused on the nature of recent trends and their potential consequences. But it is important to bear in mind that these are generalisations, and that sentencing differs markedly between individual courts – and between individual sentencers. Uniformity is not a realistic goal: there would have to be a high level of prescription, which might eliminate some disparities but introduce others by denying sentencers the discretion to take a complex mix of factors into account and deal with exceptional cases in exceptional ways. It is the rigidity of most statutory guidelines that has attracted criticism of many of the guideline systems, such as those operating in many US states which sometimes lock sentencers into having to make decisions they consider unjust (Freed and Miller, 1989 and 1990). But that does not mean that the search for greater consistency of approach should be abandoned.

Criminal Statistics England and Wales 1996 shows that the use of immediate custody in courts within different police force areas ranged between two per cent and 29 per cent of cases involving offenders aged between 18 and 20, and between one per cent and 37 per cent of cases involving offenders aged 21 and over. Analysis of sentencing data by the Research and Statistics Directorate shows that the variation in sentencing increased from 1994 to 1995 (Home Office, 1996). The Prison Reform Trust (1997) has argued that sentencing is a geographical lottery, and has published tables of proportionate use of prison and average sentence lengths in magistrates' courts to make its point. The stark fact is that where the case is heard does have a significant influence on the likelihood of custody in borderline cases, and on the length of any custodial sentence. There are also big differences in the way non-custodial options are used, which in turn is affected by variations in policy and practice between probation areas.

A number of initiatives have attempted to reduce variation in sentencing. At a local level, some sentencers request information about their own sentencing patterns so that they can compare them either to other courts in the area or to national sentencing statistics. A few magistrates' courts have carried out 'sentencing audits' where the sentencing of individual benches is compared with that of other benches within the same court. Since 1990, the Home Office Research and Statistics Directorate, the Magistrates' Association and the Justices' Clerks' Society have produced a booklet entitled *'Local sentencing patterns in magistrates' courts'*. This provides information for 12 offence types on the use of immediate custody, average length of sentence and the use of community sentences. Information is also shown on the proportionate use of disqualification from driving and the period of disqualification. It allows Justices' Clerks and magistrates to find out how sentencing in 'their' court compares with that in other magistrates' courts and is used in training.

At a national level, the Magistrates' Association's guidelines (1997) aim to reduce disparity by providing entry points for sentencing in a range of common offences. Adjustments to the guidelines are intended to reflect local circumstances. The size of recommended fines may be altered to allow for average local incomes but can go further than this. For example, one court in this sample had changed the entry point for assault from a community sentence to custody. In another area, the entry point for possession of a Class B drug had been altered from a fine to a community sentence because magistrates were concerned about what they saw as a particular local problem.

These findings are consistent with earlier research. For example, Tarling (1979) found that 20 out of 24 participating courts had adapted the guidelines (then confined to motoring offences) with the result that there was no consensus about the appropriate starting point. Courts viewed the guideline penalty as a means of achieving consistency within their own bench and only secondarily, if at all, as a method to achieve consistency between areas. Only about half of the participating courts had consulted with their neighbours in setting their own norms.

Conclusions

Questions about the need to punish offenders in order to mark society's disapproval, to protect the public from those who pose particular dangers or have a particularly high level of offending and to retain public confidence are for political and judicial consideration. However, there are points which emerged from interviews which, coupled with the evidence of sentencing practice from both official statistics and the more detailed data provided by this study suggest options which would be worth exploring further. Some of these are already under consideration. It is a reasonable assumption that most people – both the public and sentencers – would be strongly influenced in their view as to the appropriate non-custodial options by what they cost and what they achieve in terms of reparation, rehabilitation and deterrence. Reconviction rates are part of the picture, but are incomplete. For example, most offences do not result in conviction, and the nature of offending may change even when its extent does not. If some probation schemes require greater resources but achieve more, as some evidence suggests, then there may be a case for reversing the decline in the use of fines partly in order to release probation resources for more effective intervention with fewer offenders.

So far as promoting consistency is concerned, there is a clear case for more comprehensive guidance. Although the basic associations between case factors and sentences showed that factors did exert the kind of influence one would expect, the attempts to predict sentences on the basis of case factors were not particularly successful. In particular, the model which sought to predict which community penalty would be imposed having regard to case factors achieved a low success rate. This suggests wide differences in the way these sentences are used, and a need for a further assessment of aims coupled with more rigorous measurement of results.

The results of this study need to be considered alongside other recent work, such as the study of sentencing of women (Hedderman and Gelsthorpe, 1997). Where the aim is to prevent reoffending – rather than simply to punish or to protect the public – what is achieved by different sentences needs to be considered alongside costs. The detailed information as to the factors which guide sentencers in their choice between sentences will inform debate as to how practice might most usefully evolve to secure more in the way of crime reduction within the limited resources available. Looking at the trends and current patterns in respect of non-custodial sentences, the point that stands out is that the resources of the probation service appear to be dissipated on some offenders for whom a fine would serve as well.

Appendix A Methodology

The study drew on court records for such details as criminal history, social factors, value involved in the offence, whether the offender was in breach of an earlier sentence, whether the offence was committed while on bail, etc. Pre-sentence reports were also consulted, both to supplement the social information available from police antecedents (which can be out of date by the time a case reaches court) and to see what sentencing options were considered in the reports.

Pilot work undertaken for an earlier study in the Crown Court (Moxon, 1988) indicated that important information was not available from court records. In particular, mitigating and aggravating factors would often be missed unless an observer was present to hear the defence and prosecution's representations. These data were collected by researchers at magistrates' courts, who were present in court to observe court appearances in which sentencing took place; probation officers were present in 13 of 18 Crown Courts and Home Office staff at the other five Crown Courts. Only the sentencing hearing was observed as the study relied upon court records for details of previous action. Previous work in the Crown Court had found that court records were often very detailed but, in magistrates' courts, files held very little information about the offender, the offence or the previous progress of the case. This was particularly true where the offender was sentenced for a relatively minor offence (e.g. road traffic or other summary offence) after pleading guilty at the first or second appearance: in these cases the file would only contain a sheet prepared by the police specifying the charge(s) against the defendant.

On average, more than 6,000 people are sentenced each day at magistrates' courts and so collecting the data presented a number of problems. Because there was particular interest in studying the custody threshold and also in community penalties, it was decided not to take a random sample of sentenced cases.[1] Most magistrates' courts will have several court rooms running simultaneously dealing with different types of work and observers were instructed to omit courts that solely dealt with traffic offences. Where possible, they concentrated on cases which resulted in custody or a

---

[1] Most summary motoring offences were excluded from the sample. Nine out of 10 summary motoring cases result in a fine.

community penalty. This resulted in a sample which over-represents cases which resulted in custody or a community penalty, and so is focused on the more serious end of the offences that are dealt with at magistrates' courts. *The magistrates courts sample should not be seen as representative of all cases that appeared at magistrates courts. Rather, it should be interpreted as providing examples of sentencing decisions which took place in magistrates' courts.*

Data collection took place between July 1994 and May 1995 at 25 magistrates' courts in England and Wales. Fieldwork lasted for six to eight weeks at each court. After some preliminary analysis of the statistical data had taken place, the second stage of the study was to interview Justices' Clerks and magistrates at 12 of the 25 courts. The purpose of the interviews was to discuss the initial results and to ask magistrates about some of the other issues that had arisen both from this study and other work that the Research and Statistics Directorate has undertaken in this area.[2] A total of 126 magistrates took part in interviews in 28 groups. Between three and five magistrates were present at each. The study therefore uses both statistical information from the survey and interview data from magistrates' groups. Table A.1 shows a profile of the cases in the sample.

Table A.1 Profile of cases in the magistrates' courts' sample

	Number	%
Sex		
Male	2,542	84.6
Female	459	15.3
Not known	4	0.1
Age		
Under 18	21	0.7
18–21	622	20.7
22–30	1,178	39.2
31–40	624	20.8
41–50	242	8.1
51–60	97	3.2
61 and over	33	1.1
Not known	188	6.2

---

2   Magistrates and Justices' Clerks were also asked about the reasons for delays and about the enforcement of financial penalties.

Ethnic group

White	2,338	77.8
Black	335	11.1
Asian	209	7.0
Other	58	1.9
Not Known	65	2.1

Previous convictions

0	945	31.4
1-5	661	22.0
6-10	224	7.5
11-15	125	4.2
16-20	73	2.4
21 and over	91	3.0
Exact number not known	471	15.7
No information	415	13.8

Offence type

Violent	143	4.8
Sex	9	0.3
Burglary	81	2.7
Fraud and forgery	79	2.6
Theft	547	18.2
Criminal damage	139	4.6
Drug	169	5.6
Other indictable	66	2.2
Motoring	1,175	39.1
Summary non-motoring	593	19.7
Not known	4	0.1

Sentences

Immediate custody	298	10.0
Suspended custody	10	0.3
Combination order	59	2.0
CSO	194	6.5
Probation (with additional requirements)	78	2.6
Probation (without additional requirements)	206	6.9
Attendance centre orders	3	0.1
Fine	1,678	56.0
Conditional discharge	368	12.2
Absolute discharge	26	0.9
Other	79	2.6
Not known	6	0.2

Total number of cases	3,005	

Data collection took place between September 1995 and February 1996 at 18 Crown Court Centres in England and Wales. A target was set of 150 cases from each centre at which point data collection ceased. Some areas did not reach this target within the six month period.

Table A.2 shows a profile of the offenders in the Crown Court. Table A.3 shows that the sample closely resembled the national sentencing figures for 1995.

Table A.2 A profile of offenders in the Crown Court sample

	No.	%
Sex		
Men	1,596	90
Women	178	10
Not known	3	0.2
Age group		
under 17	31	2
18–20	320	18
21–30	753	42
31–40	405	23
41–50	125	7
51–60	53	3
61 and over	25	1
Not known	65	4
Ethnic group		
White	1,296	73
Black	313	18
Asian	76	4
Other	46	3
Not known	46	3
Number previous convictions		
0	528	30
1–5	571	32
6–10	240	14
11 and over	310	17
Exact number not known	69	4
No information	59	3

Table A.3 A comparison of the sample with national sentencing statistics for the Crown Court in 1995

	Sample n	Survey[1] %	National[2] %
Immediate custody	1,020	57	56
Suspended sentence	45	3	3
Community sentence	589	33	30
Fine	60	3	5
Discharge	37	2	5
Otherwise dealt with	26	2	1
Total number	1,777		71,600

Note:
1. Source : Crown Court survey
2. Source: Criminal Statistics 1995, Table 7B

Appendix B: Magistrates' court additional tables

Table B.1 Sentence by offence group (Courts' survey)

	Custody Penalty		Community sentences		Fines or discharges		Other	
	n	%	n	%	n	%	n	%
Violence	21	15	45	32	59	41	18	13
Sexual	1	11	1	11	6	67	1	11
Burglary	12	15	46	57	21	26	2	3
Fraud /deception	7	9	30	38	40	51	2	3
Theft	67	13	144	26	321	59	15	3
Criminal damage	4	3	21	15	96	69	18	13
Drug	3	2	12	7	152	90	2	1
Other indictable	4	6	16	24	44	67	2	3
Motoring	156	13	184	16	824	70	11	1
Summary – non-motoring	23	4	41	7	506	85	23	43
Total	298	10	540	18	2,072	69	95	3

Table B.2 Comparison of the sample and Criminal Statistics 1995 (All offences)

	Courts sample[1]		Criminal Statistics, 1995	
	n	%	n[2]	%
Custody	298	9.9	38.8	3.0
Suspended custody	10	0.3	1.3	0.1
Combination order	59	20.0	11.6	0.9
CSO	194	6.5	37.8	2.9
Probation	284	9.5	41.0	3.2
Supervision order	---	---	9.7	0.8
Attendance centre	3	0.1	7.4	0.6
Fine	1,678	56.0	992.8	77.6
Conditional discharge	368	12.3	102.0	8.0
Absolute discharge	26	0.9	20.1	1.6
Other	79	2.6	17.6	1.4
Total	2,999	100	1280.1	100

Note:
1. Information missing on 6 cases
2. Number in 1000s.

The factors shown in Tables B.3, B.4, B.5, B.6, B.7, B.11 and B.13 were initially identified by bivariate analysis as being associated with a higher or lower probability of custody. The multivariate technique of logistic regression was then used to identify those factors which had an independent effect upon the likelihood of custody. This technique was used because it will identify factors which, although occurring very rarely, are influential in those cases in which they do appear.

Table B.3 Offence-related factors associated with the use of custodial sentences (Magistrates' courts' survey)

Factors associated with a higher or lower use of immediate custody	No. Cases where the factor was present	% custody
Risk to the public	76	33
Vulnerable victim	8	25
Victim received a serious injury	38	26
Planned /premeditated	55	24
Uncooperative /aggressive to police	197	24
Unprovoked	52	23
Ringleader	7	14
Victim received a minor injury	120	13
Value above £200	247	13
Value less than £200	440	9
Not particular danger to the public	2,929	9
Co-operated with the police	2,808	9

Table B.4 Factors associated with the use of custodial sentences in offences of violence (Magistrates' courts' survey)

Factors associated with a higher or lower use of immediate custody	No. cases where the factor was present	% custody
Subject to another court order	30	37
Victim is police or another person in authority	23	30
More serious injuries	28	21
Previous convictions for violence	37	22
Having previous convictions	95	20
Victim is a stranger	37	19
Previous convictions not for violence	33	12
Offender under 40	117	17
Minor injuries caused	71	12
Victim is partner, relative or friend	71	8
Not subject to another court order	113	9
Offender over 40	19	5
First offender	48	4
Total violent offences	143	15

Table B.5 Factors associated with the use of custodial sentences in burglary cases (Magistrates' court's survey)

Factors associated with a higher or lower use of immediate custody	No. cases where the factor was present	% custody
Offence premeditated	5	40
Loss more than £200	27	30
Subject to a court order at the time	26	27
More than five previous convictions	47	23
Burglary of a private dwelling	28	21
Burglary of a commercial property	36	11
Not subject to a court order at the time of the current offence	55	9
Spontaneous	12	8
Loss less than £200	43	7
Five or under previous convictions	34	3
Total of burglary cases	81	15

Table B.6 Factors associated with the use of custodial sentences in offences of theft (Magistrates' courts survey)

Factors associated with a higher or lower use of immediate custody	No. cases where the factor was present	% custody
Subject to another court order	186	24
Theft of /from a vehicle	28	20
Sentenced for more than one offence	258	19
Previous convictions for theft	308	17
Did not offer compensation or show remorse	366	16
Offences taken into consideration	48	15
Previous convictions	444	15
Aged less than 30	362	14
No offences taken into consideration	499	12
Previous convictions not for theft	136	10
Aged over 30	157	8
Offered compensation or otherwise showed remorse	181	7
Not subject to another court order	361	6
Sentenced for one offence	289	6
First offender	103	2
Total of theft cases	547	12

Table B.7 Factors associated with the use of community sentences rather than a fine or discharge (Magistrates' court's survey)[1]

Factors associated with a higher or lower use of immediate custody	No. cases where the factor was present	% custody
Offence involved a breach of trust	22	73
Convicted of burglary, violence or fraud	241	50
Subject to a court order at the time of the current offence	527	41
Compensation also awarded	315	40
Unco-operative with police at the time of arrest	144	40
History of similar convictions	315	38
Sentenced for more than one offence	1,150	31
Previous convictions	1,709	27
No breach of trust involved	2,590	20
Attitude to police not discussed	2,468	20
Compensation not awarded	2,297	19
Convicted of another offence type	2,371	18
Not subject to a court order at the time of current offence	2,085	16
Sentenced for one offence	1,462	12
First offence	903	8
Total number of cases	2.999	2,612

Note:
1.This table only includes those sentenced to a community sentence, a fine or a discharge.

Table B.8 Additional requirements to probation orders (Magistrates' courts' survey)

	n	% cases
Activities		
Attend a motor project	28	36
Intensive probation	12	15
Other group activity	8	10
Alcohol related treatment or counselling	15	19
Receive treatment or counselling for a drug related problem	10	13
Psychiatric treatment	5	6
Residence at a hostel	0	0
Total number	78	100

Table B.9 Actual sentence against predicted sentence: community penalties (Magistrates' courts' survey)[1]

Actual Sentence	Predicted sentence		
	Combination order %	Community service %	Probation order %
Combination order	**61**	7	32
Community Service	28	**42**	30
Probation order	27	27	**47**

Note: 1. The model produced by this discriminant analysis correctly predicted 46% of cases. Cases which did not receive a community sentence were excluded from the analysis. Attendance centre orders were excluded from this analysis because there were very few in the sample.

Table B.10 Proportion of cases which result in (a) a fine and (b) a conditional discharge in magistrates' courts (Source : Criminal Statistics 1994)

	Fine %	Conditional discharge %	Total resulting in a fine or discharge %
Non-motoring summary offences	84	9	93
Summary motoring	90	1	91
Drugs	67	19	86
Theft	36	28	64
Other indictable	39	23	62
Deception /handling	30	26	56
Criminal damage	22	33	55
Sexual	32	22	54
Violent	22	30	52
Burglary	11	15	26
Percentage all offences	79	8	87

Table B.11 Factors associated with the use of fines rather than any other sentence (Courts' survey)

Factors associated with higher or lower use of fines	No. cases where factor present	% fine
Employed	892	70
Convicted of drugs, motoring or other summary (non-motoring) offences	1,937	69
First offender	945	69
Sentenced for just one offence	1,577	65
Not in breach of previous court order	2,263	63
Compensation not awarded	2,646	59
Attitude to police not discussed	2,808	57
Unemployed	1,815	50
Previous convictions	2,060	50
Danger to the public	76	47
Sentenced for more than one offence	1,428	46
Family responsibilities		41
Mentally ill or stressed	261	34
Unco-operative/aggressive with the police	197	34
In breach of court order	742	33
Convicted of violent, sexual or property offences (including criminal damage)	998	31
Compensation awarded	359	31
Offences taken into consideration	99	19
Total number of cases	3,005	56

Table B.12 Sentencing outcome by employment status and criminal record[1] (Magistrates' courts' survey)

Offence type	First offender				Repeat offenders			
	Employed		Unemployed		Employed		Unemployed	
	n	%	n	%	n	%	n	%
Custody	4	1	6	1	54	14	170	15
Community Sentence	25	6	45	10	98	26	290	26
Fine	335	82	260	57	200	53	476	43
Discharge	39	10	125	27	17	5	146	13
Other	6	2	19	5	9	2	39	4
Total	409	100	455	100	378	100	1,121	100

Note:1. Information was missing on employment status in 642 cases.

Table B.13 Factors which were associated with likelihood of receiving a conditional discharge rather than any other sentence (Magistrates' courts' survey)

Factors associated with higher or lower use of conditional discharges	No. cases where factor was present	% conditional discharge
Compensation also awarded	359	21
Convicted of violence, fraud or criminal damage	361	26
Female offender	459	21
Mentally ill or stressed	261	19
Unemployed	1,815	15
First offender	945	17
Male offender	2,542	11
Compensation not awarded	2,646	11
Having previous convictions	2,060	10
Convicted other offences	2,644	10
Employed	892	6
Total	3,005	12

Table B.14 Compensation by offence type (Magistrates' courts' survey)[1]

	Total No.	% cases compensation awarded
Violence	121	65
Criminal damage	135	53
Sexual	8	38
Burglary	69	32
Deception/fraud	72	19
Other indictable	61	18
Theft	479	17
Summary (non-motoring)	570	6
Motoring	987	3
Total no. of cases not resulting in a custodial sentences	2,345	13

Note:
1. Cases resulting in a custodial sentence where excluded as compensation was rarely awarded alongside a custodial sentence.

Table B.15 Compensation by sentence (Magistrates' courts' survey)

	Violence		Property	
	n	%	n	%
Custody	21	10	90	2
Suspended sentence	1	100	4	40
Community sentence	45	64	241	25
Fine	31	65	277	21
Discharge	28	64	201	24
Other	17	59	33	58
Total	143	56	846	23

NOTE
1. Includes cases where a compensation order was the sole sentence.

Appendix C Sentencing by lay and stipendiary magistrates, sentencing of offenders from different ethnic groups and sentencing of men and women: Additional tables and statistical models

Table C.1   Sentencing patterns: lay and stipendiary magistrates

| | London | | | | Provinces | | | |
| | Stipendiary | | Lay | | Stipendiary | | Lay | |
	n	%	n	%	n	%	n	%
Custody	52	10	65	7	57	19	123	11
Community sentence	69	13	185	21	50	16	263	21
Fine Discharge	426	78	653	72	199	65	792	69
Total	547	100	903	100	306	100	1,178	100

Table C.2 Proportionate use of custody: lay and stipendiary magistrates in London and the Provinces

| | London | | Provinces | |
	n	% Custody	n	% Custody
Stipendiary magistrate	543	10	304	19
Lay JP in courts with a stipendiary	475	8	437	12
Lay JP in courts without a stipendiary	432	6	717	10
Total	1,450	8	1,458	12

Table C.3 Logistic regression model of type of magistrate and the likelihood of a custodial sentence

Variable	B	S.E.	Wald	df	Sig	R	Exp (B)
Male	0.5395	0.15	12.10	1	0.0005	0.0789	1.7152
Number of previous convictions	0.0086	0.002	18.71	1	0.0000	0.1015	1.0086
Similar convictions	-0.4499	0.08	29.10	1	0.0000	-0.1292	0.6377
Lay Magistrates	-0.4602	0.09	29.17	1	0.0000	-0.1294	0.6311
Not subject to earlier court order	-0.8656	0.08	110.11	1	0.0000	-0.2581	0.4208
Offence type violent/sex	-1.5603	12.58	0.02	1	0.9013	0.0000	0.2101
Property	1.3576	3.15	0.19	1	0.6668	0.0000	3.8868
Summary – non motoring	-0.3424	3.15	0.01	1	0.9134	0.0000	1.4083
Summary – motoring	-0.6751	3.15	0.05	1	0.8304	0.0000	0.5091
Number of offences	0.3926	0.05	65.25	1	0.0000	0.1974	1.4809
Constant	-3.7959	3.15	1.45	1	0.2284		

Table C.4 Sentencing of men by ethnicity at magistrates' courts

	White		Black		Asian	
	n	%	n	%	n	%
Custody	224	11	30	11	21	11
Community sentence	383	20	48	17	18	9
Fine	1,055	54	168	59	133	69
Discharge	243	86	24	8	15	8
Other	58	3	16	6	5	3
Total	1,963	100	286	100	192	100

Table C.5 Sentencing of first offenders by ethnicity (Men only) (Crown Court survey)

	White		Black		Asian	
	n	%	n	%	n	%
Immediate custody	129	48	33	45	13	46
Suspended custody	6	2	0	0	0	0
Combination order	25	9	3	4	1	4
CSO	57	21	24	33	9	32
Probation	24	9	6	8	0	0
Fine	18	7	4	6	2	7
Conditional discharge	6	2	2	3	3	11
Other	3	1	1	1	0	0
Total	268	100	73	100	28	100

Note:
Data on ethnic group was only available from 17 of the 18 Crown Court centres

Table C.6 Sentencing of offenders with previous convictions by ethnicity (Men only) (Crown Court survey)

	White		Black		Asian	
	n	%	n	%	n	%
Immediate custody	454	64	104	62	20	69
Suspended custody	15	2	1	1	0	0
Combination order	42	6	11	7	2	7
CSO	94	13	22	13	4	14
Probation	75	11	20	12	1	3
Fine	15	2	4	2	1	3
Conditional discharge	7	1	2	1	1	3
Other	10	1	5	3	0	0
Total	712	100	169	100	29	100

Note:
Data on ethnic group was only available from 17 of the 18 Crown Court centres

Table C.7 Logistic regression model of race and likelihood of a custodial sentence (magistrates' court survey)

Variable	B	S.E.	Wald	df	Sig	R	Exp (B)
Remand status			44.4657	2	0.0000	0.1713	
Bail	-0.6367	0.1604	15.7589	1	0.0001	-0.0999	0.5290
Custody	0.7633	0.1708	19.9681	1	0.0000	0.1142	2.1454
Race			6.4982	2	0.0388	0.0426	
Asian	0.5095	0.2233	5.2603	1	0.0225	0.0482	1.6645
Black	-0.2022	0.2034	0.9878	1	0.3203	0.0000	0.8170
No previous convictions	-0.8985	0.2020	19.7842	1	0.0000	-0.1136	0.4072
No PSR	-1.3182	0.1401	88.4730	1	0.0000	-0.2505	0.2676
Lay magistrate	-0.3699	0.0980	14.2368	1	0.0002	-0.0942	0.6908
Number offences	0.2772	0.0558	24.6725	1	0.0000	0.1283	1.3194
Offence type			14.6217	5	0.0121	0.0579	
Violent sex	0.5577	0.3284	2.8842	1	0.0895	0.0253	1.7466
Property	-0.0134	0.2189	0.0038	1	0.9511	0.0000	0,9867
Drugs	-1.1937	0.6511	3.3610	1	0.0668	-0.0314	0.3031
Summary non-motoring	0.3626	0.2840	1.6304	1	0.2016	0.0000	1.4371
Summary motoring	0.5888	0.1999	8.6721	1	0.0032	0.0696	1.8018
Constant	-3.4192	0.292	136.4648	1	0.0000		

Table C.8 Proportionate use of custody by offence type and sex (Magistrates' court's survey)

| | First offenders | | | | Recidivists | | | |
| | Males | | Females | | Males | | Females | |
	Total no.	% cust.	Total no.	% cust.	Total no.	% cust.	Total no.	% cust.
Violence and sex	41	2	10	10	92	22	9	0
Property	140	1	64	3	546	16	95	8
Other indictable	58	0	10	0	160	5	11	0
Summary – non-motoring	171	1	17	0	245	8	159	1
Summary – motoring	383	1	50	2	706	21	34	6
Total	793	1	151	3	1,749	16	308	4

Table C.9 Logistic regression model of sex and likelihood of a custodial sentence at the magistrates' court

1 = custody
0 = non - custodial sentence

Variable	B	S.E.	Wald	df	Sig	R	Exp (B)
Lay magistrates	-0.3355	0.0807	17.2807	1	0.0000	-0.0929	0.7150
Offence type	21.0294		5.0008		0.0789		
Violence sex	0.9123	0.2850	10.2472	1	0.0014	0.0682	2.4900
Property	0.1939	0.2021	0.9204	1	0.3374	0.0000	1.2139
Drugs	-1.5398	0.6286	6.0010	1	0.0143	-0.0475	0.2144
Summary non – motoring	-0.0834	0.2620	0.1014	1	0.7501	0.0000	0.9199
Summary motoring	0.6277	0.1951	10.3472	1	0.0013	0.0686	1.8732
Remand status			101.4424	2	0.0000	0.2345	
Bail	-0.0992	0.1236	0.6443	1	0.4222	0.0000	0.9055
Custody	1.4761	0.1498	97.0461	1	0.0000	0.2316	4.3758
Male	0.4031	0.1549	6.7769	1	0.0092	0.0519	1.4965
No previous convictions	-0.7640	0.1597	22.8987	1	0.0000	-0.1086	0.4658
Number of offences	0.3155	0.0460	46.9812	1	0.0000	0.1594	1.3709
No similar PC	-0.3288	0.0797	17.0141	1	0.0000	0.7198	
Constant	-3.9917	0.2869	193.5784	1	0.0000		

Table C.10 Logistic regression model showing the influence of the race of the offender[1] (Crown Court Survey)

Variable	B	S.E.	Wald	df	Sig	R	Exp (B)
Remand in custody	0.7440	0.0766	104.84	1	****	0.2501	2.1902
Offence types			45.16	9	****	0.1285	
Violence	0.0568	0.1637	0.1202	1	****	0.0000	1.0584
Sex	1.3795	0.3969	12.08	1	****	0.0783	3.9729
Robbery	0.6474	0.2900	4.99	1	****	0.0426	1.9106
Burglary	-0.0309	0.1815	0.03	1	****	0.0000	0.9696
Fraud and forgery	-0.1363	0.2104	0.42	1	****	0.0000	0.8726
Theft	-0.6202	0.1673	13.75	1	****	-0.0845	0.5378
Drug	0.2780	0.1754	2.51	1	****	0.0176	1.3204
Public order	-0.9859	0.2629	14.06	1	****	-0.0856	0.3731
Other	-0.2961	0.3182	0.87	1	****	0.0000	0.7437
Offence not	0.2475	0.0906	7.47	1	****	0.0577	1.2808
spontaneous	0.2475	0.0906	7.47	1	****	0.0577	1.2808
Subject to							
a court order	0.2269	0.0870	6.80	1	****	0.0540	1.2547
Plea			5.31	2	****	0.0282	
Guilty	-0.0542	0.1870	0.0841	1	****	0.0000	0.9472
Not guilty	0.3052	0.1964	2.41	1	****	0.0159	1.3569
Number offences	0.0590	0.0381	2.40	1	****	0.0156	1.0608
Not mentally ill	0.1207	0.0801	2.27	1	****	0.0128	1.1283
Ethnic origin		0	1.72	2	****	0.0000	
White	0.0092	0.1255	0.01	1	****	0.0000	1.0092
Black	-0.1934	0.1508	1.64	1	****	0.0000	0.8242
Court outside							
London	0.0833	0.0706	1.39	1	****	0.0000	1.0869
Age	0.0068	0.0077	0.79	1	****	0.0000	1.0068
Number previous							
convictions	0.0069	0.0083	0.69	1	****	0.0000	1.0070
Constant	0.1288	0.3160	0.1661	1		0.6836	

Note:
1. This model correctly predicted the outcome in 70% of cases in the sample. The ethnicity of the offender was omitted
   from the best fitting model.
2. *** significant at 5% level; ** significant at 10% level; —- not significant at 10% level

Table C.11 Sentencing of men and women (Crown Court survey)

| | First offenders | | | | Previous convictions | | | |
| | Men | | Women | | Men | | Women | |
	n	%	n	%	n	%	n	%
Immediate custody	209	48	40	42	730	63	40	49
Suspended custody	9	2	10	10	20	2	6	7
Community sentence	167	39	32	33	351	30	35	43
Fine	29	7	1	1	29	3	1	1
Conditional discharge	11	3	9	9	17	2	0	0
Other	7	2	4	4	17	2	0	0
Total	432	100	96	100	1,164	100	82	100

Table C.12 Logistic regression model showing the influence of the sex of the offender[1]

Variable	B	S.E.	Wald	df	Sig	R	Exp (B)
Offence type			96.54	9		0.1999	
Violence	0.2568	0.1418	3.28	1	**	0.0255	1.2929
Sex	1.5873	0.3533	20.18	1	***	0.0962	4.8904
Robbery	0.7070	0.2361	8.97	1	***	0.0596	2.0279
Burglary	0.1479	0.1580	0.88	1	---	0.0000	1.1594
Fraud and forgery	-0.3021	0.1696	3.17	1	**	-0.0244	0.7393
Theft	-0.8233	0.1452	32.15	1	***	-0.1239	0.4390
Drug	0.3353	0.1520	4.87	1	***	0.0382	1.3984
Public order	-1.1628	0.2360	24.27	1		-0.1065	0.3126
Other	-0.3853	0.2759	1.95	1	---	0.0000	
Number of previous convictions	0.0208	0.0073	8.14	1	***	0.0559	1.0210
Number of offences	0.1185	0.0340	12.12	1	***	0.0718	1.1258
Male	0.2089	0.0933	5.01	1	***	0.0391	1.2323
Subject to a court order	0.3155	0.0730	18.65	1	***	0.0921	1.3709
Not mentally ill	0.1530	0.0676	5.12	1	***	0.0399	1.1653
Offences not spontaneous	0.2726	0.0802	11.57	1	***	0.0698	1.3134
Constant	-0.3107	0.1466	4.4922	1	***		

Note:
1. This model correctly predicted the outcome in 65 % of cases in the sample.
2. *** significant at 5 % level; ** significant at 10 % level; — not significant at 10 % level.

Appendix D Additional tables from the Crown Court

Table D.1 Sentencing by age (Crown Court survey)

| | First offenders | | | | Previous convictions | | | |
| | 18–20 years | | 21 years | | 18–20 years | | 21 years and over | |
	n	%	n	%	n	%	n	%
Immediate custody	48	41	190	49	146	62	598	61
Suspended custody[1]	n/a	n/a	18	5	n/a	n/a	25	3
Combination order	11	9	23	6	21	9	50	5
Community service	29	25	82	21	21	9	138	14
Probation	13	11	30	8	35	15	114	12
Fine	3	3	26	7	0	0	28	3
Conditional discharge	4	3	16	4	3	1	13	1
Other[2]	9	8	2	1	8	3	8	1
Total	117	100	387	100	234	100	974	100

Note:
1. Suspended sentences are not available to persons below 21
2. 'Other' includes attendance centre orders, compensation orders as the main sentence, and hospital orders.

Table D.2 Proportionate use of immediate custody by number of previous convictions

	n	% immediate custody
0	528	47
1–5	571	58
6–10	240	63
11–15	124	71
16–20	83	72
21 and over	231	62
Total	1,777	57

Table D.3 Proportionate use of immediate custody by whether offender was in breach of a particular court order (Crown Court survey)

	n	% immediate custody
Suspended sentence	20	55
Release on licence	52	71
Community sentence	221	71
Conditional discharge	55	60
On bail	57	74
Other court order	28	68
Not in breach of a court order	1,227	53
Total	1,660	57

Note:
Information missing from 119 cases

Table D.4 Proportionate use of immediate custody by remand status (Crown Court survey)

	First offenders		Previous convictions	
	n	% custody	n	% custody
Bail	390	36	660	44
Remand	111	90	488	85
In prison on other charges	n/a	n/a	41	83
Total	501	48	1,189	63

Note:
Information missing in 87 cases.

Table D.5 Sentencing by offence
(Crown Court survey)

	Custody		Community		Fine or sentence		Other discharge	
	n	%	n	%	n	%	n	%
Violence	171	59	104	36	15	5	2	1
Sex	69	86	8	10	3	3	0	0
Robbery	80	75	16	15	1	1	10	39
Burglary	187	67	86	31	3	1	3	1
Fraud	101	51	85	43	11	6	1	1
Theft	125	42	144	49	25	8	2	1
Drugs	182	66	76	28	15	6	1	1
Public order	34	32	55	52	13	12	4	4
Motoring	41	51	32	40	6	8	1	1
Other	29	46	27	43	5	8	2	3
Total	1,019	57	633	36	97	6	26	2

The factors shown in Tables D.7, D.8, D.9, D.10, D.11, D.12, D.13, D.14, D.15 and D.18 were initially identified by bivariate analysis as being associated with a higher or lower probability of custody. The multivariate technique of logistic regression was then used to identify those factors which had an independent effect upon the likelihood of custody. This technique was used because it will identify factors which, although occurring very rarely, are influential in those cases in which they do appear.

Table D.6 Factors associated with the use of immediate custodial sentences (Crown Court survey)

Factors associated with a higher or lower use of immediate custody	No. of cases where factor present	% Custody
Offence involved a breach of trust	116	72
Planned /premeditated	459	72
Unprovoked	198	71
Ringleader	86	70
Vulnerable victim	19	68
Weapon used	196	67
Under the influence of drugs at time of offence	212	67
Mentally ill or under stress	417	51
Spontaneous	304	46
Minor role in offence	216	43
Provoked	132	42
Total all offences	1,777	57

Table D.7 Violent offences: Factors associated with the use of immediate custodial sentences (Crown Court survey)

Factors associated with a higher or lower use of immediate custody	No. of cases where factor present	% Custody
Sentenced for manslaughter or GBH's18	45	91
Premeditated	50	84
Serious injury caused	116	75
Previous good character not mentioned in court	156	64
Unemployed	172	64
Offender said to be of previously good character	136	53
Other violent offence	246	53
Employed	100	47
Minor injury caused to the victim	50	40
Total number of violent offences	292	59

Table D.8 Robbery offences: Factors associated with the use of immediate custodial sentences (Crown Court survey)

Factors associated with a higher or lower use of immediate custody	No. of cases where factor present	% Custody
Subject to a court order at the time of current offence	34	91
Ringleader	8	88
Convicted of more than one offence	48	85
Previous convictions	70	84
Any injury caused	25	80
Not subject to a court order at time of current offence	67	66
Convicted of one offence only	66	66
First offender	37	57
Mentally ill	22	59
Minor role on the offence	9	44
Total number of robbery offences	107	75

Table D.9 Burglary: Factors associated with the use of immediate custodial sentences (Crown Court survey)

Factors associated with a higher or lower use of immediate custody	No. of cases where factor present	% Custody
Any injury was caused to victim	24	92
Large amount of money involved	41	885
Remanded in custody	156	81
Offender has previous convictions	247	72
Burglary of a dwelling	181	72
Burglary of commercial property	93	57
Offender has financial problems	62	57
On bail prior to sentencing	48	48
First offender	32	31
Total number of burglary offences	279	67

Table D.10 Theft offences: Factors associated with the use of immediate custodial sentences (Crown Court survey)

Factors associated with a higher or lower use of immediate custody	No. of cases where factor present	% Custody
Asian offender	13	69
Theft of more than £1,000	119	57
Subject to a court order at time of current offence	81	57
Previous convictions for theft	164	51
Male offender	261	46
Not subject to a court order at time of current offence	198	35
Amount involved in offence less than £1,000	177	32
Offender was mentally ill	68	31
No previous convictions for theft	36	22
Female offender	33	18
Total number of theft offences	296	42

Table D.11 Factors associated with the use of immediate custodial sentences (Crown Court survey)

Factors associated with a higher or lower use of immediate custody	No. of cases where factor present	% Custody
Remanded in custody	98	95
Large amount of drugs involved	32	94
Pleaded not guilty	63	4
Supplying drugs	208	76
Pleaded guilty	206	61
On bail prior to sentencing	160	49
Change in circumstances since offence	19	37
Possession of drugs	64	34
Total number of drugs offences	274	66

Table D.12 ***Proportion of cases receiving an immediate custodial sentence over 18 months by factors related to the offence (Crown Court survey)[1]***

Factors associated with longer sentences	No. of cases where factor present	% receiving over 18 months sentence
Ringleader	58	64
Weapon used in offence	128	64
Premeditated offence	322	58
Did not express any remorse	115	54
Victim was injured	201	47
Spontaneous	139	27
Total number of cases resulting in immeidate custody	1,020	42

Note:

1. Excludes cases which did not receive an immediate custodial sentence. Eighteen months was chosen because all broad categories of offences had some cases either side of this dividing line. A higher limit would have excluded some of the less serious offences dealt with by the Crown Court few of which received a sentence greater than 18 months.

Table D.13 Proportion of cases receiving an immediate custodial sentence over 18 months by factors related to the offender (Crown Court survey)[1]

Factors associated with longer sentences	No. of cases where factor present	% receiving sentence longer than 18 months
No pre-sentence report available	146	63
Pleaded not guilty	284	55
Aged 21 or over	772	46
Male offender	924	44
Unemployed	681	44
Pre-sentence report available	836	40
Pleaded guilty	689	39
Employed	251	37
Caring for a dependent relative	168	34
Change in personal circumstances since the offence	79	32
Aged under 21	193	31
Female	77	29
Committed for sentence from magistrates' court	19	21
Total number of cases receiving custodial sentence	1,020	42

Note:
1. Excludes cases which did not receive an immediate custodial sentence

Table D.14 *Factors associated with the use of a community sentence*

Factors associated with longer sentences	No. of cases where factor present	% community service
Spontaneous offence	304	45
Theft, fraud or public order offence	600	43
Sentenced for one offence	896	38
Aged under 21	351	38
Offender mentally ill	417	37
Offender not mentally ill	1,360	32
Aged 21 and over	1,361	32
Another type of offence	1,177	28
Sentenced for more than one offence	846	22
Offence involved large amount of loss/damage	210	22
Premeditated offence	459	21
Offence involved a breach of trust	116	19
Total number of all cases	1,777	33

Table D.15 *Actual Sentence against predicted sentence according: community penalties. (Crown Court survey)*

	Predicted sentence		
Actual Sentence	Combination order %	Community service %	Probation order %
Combination order	**36**	33	32
Community service	18	**73**	11
Probation order	27	24	**49**

Note:
1. The model produced by this discriminant analysis predicted 54% of cases correctly.

Table D.16 Proportionate use of the fine in the Crown Court survey

	n	% fined	Average (median) fine (£)
Violence	292	3	150
Sex	82	3	750
Robbery	107	0	---
Burglary	279	1	175
Fraud	198	3	250
Theft[1]	296	4	225
Drugs	274	4	225
Public order	106	9	250
Motoring[2]	80	6	400
Other	63	3	150
Total	1,777	3	250

Table D.17 Factors associated with the use of a fine rather than another type of sentence

Factors associated with high use of fines	No. cases where factor present	% fined
Employed	529	8
First offender	528	6
Aged over 21	1,361	4
Male offender	1,596	4
Premeditated	459	2
Has previous convictions	1,249	2
Offender mentally ill	417	2
Unemployed	1,147	1
Subject to a court order at the time of current offence	446	1
Aged under 21	351	1
Offender addicted to drugs or alcohol	212	1
Female offender	178	1
Large value property/loss involved	210	0
Offence involved a breach of trust	116	0
Total	1,777	3

Note:
This table is based on bivariate analysis. All the factors reported were associated with the use of a fine rather than any other sentence at the 5% significance level.

Table D.18 *Sentencing of offenders by employment status and previous convictions*

| | First offenders | | | | Previous convictions | | | |
| | Employed | | Unemployed | | Employed | | Unemloyed | |
	n	%	n	%	n	%	n	%
Immediate custody	104	45	134	48	151	50	561	5
Suspended custody	6	3	12	4	9	3	17	2
Combination order	12	5	23	8	21	7	48	6
CSO	68	30	49	18	73	24	86	10
Probation	6	3	37	13	25	8	118	14
Fine	22	10	6	2	18	6	10	1
Conditional discharge	9	4	10	4	2	1	12	1
Other	2	1	8	3	1	0.3	16	2
Total	229	100	279	100	300	100	868	100

References

Ashworth, A., (1992) *Sentencing and Criminal Justice* London: Weidenfeld and Nicholson

Ashworth, A., and Hough M., (1996) *'Sentencing and the climate of opinion'* Criminal Law Review pp. 776–86

Barker, M., (1993) *Community service and women offenders.* Association of Chief Officers of Probation

Charles N., Whittaker, C. and Ball, C., (1997) *Sentencing without a pre-sentence report* Home Office Research and Statistics Directorate Research Findings No. 47 London: Home Office

Charman, E., Gibson, B., Honess, T. and Morgan, R., (1996) *Imposition of fines following the Criminal Justice Act 1993* Home Office Research Findings No 34 London: Home Office

Commission for Racial Equality, (1992) *Juvenile Cautioning: Ethnic monitoring in practice*

Ellis, T., Hedderman, C., and Mortimer, E., (1996) *Enforcing community sentences* Home Office Research Study No. 158 London: Home Office

Ekblom, P., Law, H., and Sutton, M., (1996) *Domestic burglary schemes in the safer cities programme* Home Office Research Findings No. 42

FitzGerald, M., (1993) *Ethnic minorities and the criminal justice system* Royal Commission on Criminal Justice Research Study No. 20

Freed, D. J., and Miller, M., (1989) (Eds) *Federal sentencing reporter* Vol 2 no 6 Dec 1989/Jan 1990 pp. 185-191, Vera Institute of Justice

Freed, D. J., and Miller, M., (1990) (Eds) *Federal sentencing reporter* Vol 3 no 1 June/July pp. 3-7, Vera Institute of Justice

Gelsthorpe, L. and Loukes, N., (1997) 'Magistrates' explanations of sentencing decisions' in Hedderman, C. and Gelsthorpe, L. (eds) (1997) *Understanding the sentencing of women* Home Office Research Study No. 170. London: Home Office

Hamilton. J. and Wisniewski, M., (1996) *The use of the compensation order in Scotland* Edinburgh: The Scottish Office Central Research Unit

Hedderman, C. and Moxon, A. D., (1992) *Magistrates' court or Crown Court: mode of trial decisions and sentencing* Home Office Research Study No. 125. London: HMSO

Hedderman, C. and Gelsthorpe, L., (1997) *Understanding the sentencing of women* Home Office Research Study No 170. London: Home Office

Henham, R., (1996) Sentencing policy, appeallate guidance and prtective sentencing *Journal of Criminal Law* Vol. 60 No. 2 May 1986 pp, 208-215

Home Office (1990) *Crime and protecting the public* London: Home Office

Home Ofice, Department of Health, Welsh Office (1995) *National Standards for the supervision of ofenders in the community.* London: Home Office

Hood R., with Cordovil, G., (1992) *Race and sentencing: a study in the Crown Court.* A report for the Commission for Racial Equality Oxford: Clarendon Press

HMI Probation, (1995) *Probation orders with additional requirements: report of a thematic inspection* London: Home Office

Lloyd, C., Mair, G., and Hough, J. M., (1995) *Explaining reconviction rates: a critical analysis.* Home Office Research Study No 136. London HMSO

Mair, G., Sibbitt, R. and Crisp, D., (1995) *Combination orders: an interim report* (unpublished report to the Home Office).

Mair, G. and May, C., (1997) *Offenders on probation* Home Office Research Study No. 167. London: Home Office

Morgan P., and Pearce, R., (1989) *Remand decisions in Brighton and Bournemouth* Reseach and Planning Unit Paper No. 53 London: Home Office

Morgan, R. and Clarkson C., (1995) 'The politics of sentencing reform' in Morgan, R. and Clarkson, C. (eds) *The politics of sentencing reform* Oxford: Clarendon Press

Moxon, A.D., (1988) *Sentencing practice in the Crown Court.* Home Office Research Study Number 103 London: HMSO

Moxon, D., Corkery, J. M., and Hedderman, C., (1992) *Developments in the use of compensation in Magistrates' courts since October 1988.* Home Office Research Study No. 126 London: HMSO

Newburn, T., (1988) *The use and enforcement of compensation orders in magistrates' courts* Home Office Research Study Number 102 London: HMSO

Seago, P., Walker, C. and Wall, D., (1995) *The role and appointment of stipendiary magsitrates.* University of Leeds: Centre for Criminal Justice Studies and the Lord Chancellor's Department

Tarling, R., (1979) *Sentencing practice in magistrates' courts.* Home Office Research Study No. 56 London: HMSO

Walker, M. A., (1988) *'The court disposal of young males by race in London in 1983'* British Journal of Criminology Vol. 28 No. 4

Walker, M. A., (1989) *'The court disposal and remands of white, Afro-Caribbean and Asian men'* (London 1983)' British Journal of Criminology Vol. 29 No. 4

Wasik, M., (1993) *Emmins on sentencing* 2nd edition London: Wiedenfeld and Nicholson

Wasik, M., and von Hirsch, A., (1994) *'Section 29 revised: previous convictions in sentencing'* Criminal Law Review June pp. 409-18

Whittaker C., (1997) *Reconvictions after sentence.* Unpublished paper to the Home Office

Publications

List of research publications

A list of research reports for the last year is provided below. A **full** list of publications is available on request from the Research and Statistics Directorate Information and Publications Group.

Home Office Research Studies (HORS)

170. **Understanding the sentencing of women.** Edited by Carol Hedderman and Lorraine Gelsthorpe. 1997.

171. **Changing offenders' attitudes and behaviour: what works?** Julie Vennard, Darren Sugg and Carol Hedderman. 1997.

172. **Drug misuse declared in 1996: latest results from the British Crime Survey.** Malcolm Ramsay and Josephine Spiller. 1997.

173. **Ethnic monitoring in police forces: a beginning.** Marian FitzGerald and Rae Sibbitt. 1997.

174. **In police custody: Police powers and suspects' rights under the revised PACE codes of practice.** Tom Bucke and David Brown. 1997.

176. **The perpetrators of racial harassment and racial violence.** Rae Sibbitt. 1997.

177. **Electronic monitoring in practice: the second year of the trials of curfew orders.** Ed Mortimer and Chris May. 1997.

178. **Handling stolen goods and theft: A market reduction approach.** Mike Sutton. 1998.

179. **Attitudes to punishment: findings from the British Crime Survey.** Michael Hough and Julian Roberts. 1998.

181. **Coroner service survey.** Roger Tarling. 1998.

182. **The prevention of plastic and cheque fraud revisited.** Michael Levi and Jim Handley. 1998.

183.   **Drugs and crime: the results of research on drug testing and interviewing arrestees.** Trevor Bennett. 1998.

No. 175 is not yet published.

Research Findings

52.   **Police cautioning in the 1990s.** Roger Evans and Rachel Ellis. 1997.

53.   **A reconviction study of HMP Grendon Therapeutic Community.** Peter Marshall. 1997.

54.   **Control in category c prisons.** Simon Marshall. 1997.

55.   **The prevalence of convictions for sexual offending.** Peter Marshall. 1997.

56.   **Drug misuse declared in 1996: key results from the British Crime Survey.** Malcolm Ramsay and Josephine Spiller. 1997.

57.   **The 1996 International Crime Victimisation Survey.** Pat Mayhew and Phillip White. 1997.

58.   **The sentencing of women: a section 95 publication.** Carol Hedderman and Lizanne Dowds. 1997.

59.   **Ethnicity and contacts with the police: latest findings from the British Crime Survey.** Tom Bucke. 1997.

60.   **Policing and the public: findings from the 1996 British Crime Survey.** Catriona Mirrlees-Black and Tracy Budd. 1997.

61.   **Changing offenders' attitudes and behaviour: what works?** Julie Vennard, Carol Hedderman and Darren Sugg. 1997.

62.   **Suspects in police custody and the revised PACE codes of practice.** Tom Bucke and David Brown. 1997.

63.   **Neighbourhood watch co-ordinators.** Elizabeth Turner and Banos Alexandrou. 1997.

64.   **Attitudes to punishment: findings from the 1996 British Crime Survey.** Michael Hough and Julian Roberts. 1998.

65.   **The effects of video violence on young offenders.** Kevin Browne and Amanda Pennell. 1998.

66. **Electronic monitoring of curfew orders: the second year of the trials.** Ed Mortimer and Chris May. 1998.

67. **Public perceptions of drug-related crime in 1997.** Nigel Charles. 1998.

68. **Witness care in magistrates' courts and the youth court.** Joyce Plotnikoff and Richard Woolfson. 1998.

69. **Handling stolen goods and theft: a market reduction approach.** Mike Sutton. 1998.

70. **Drug testing arrestees.** Trevor Bennett. 1998.

71. **Prevention of plastic card fraud.** Michael Levi and Jim Handley. 1998.

72. **Offending on bail and police use of conditional bail.** David Brown. 1998.

73. **Voluntary after-care.** Mike Maguire, Peter Raynor, Maurice Vanstone and Jocelyn Kynch. 1998.

74. **Fast-tracking of persistent young offenders.** John Graham. 1998.

75. **Mandatory drug testing in prisons – an evaluation.** Kimmett Edgar and Ian O'Donnell. 1998.

Occasional Papers

Evaluation of a Home Office initiative to help offenders into employment. Ken Roberts, Alana Barton, Julian Buchanan and Barry Goldson. 1997.

The impact of the national lottery on the horse-race betting levy. Simon Field and James Dunmore. 1997.

The cost of fires. A review of the information available. Donald Roy. 1997.

Monitoring and evaluation of WOLDS remand prison and comparisons with public-sector prisons, in particular HMP Woodhill. A Keith Bottomley, Adrian James, Emma Clare and Alison Liebling. 1997.

Requests for Publications

Home Office Research Studies and Research Findings can be requested from:

Research and Statistics Directorate
Information and Publications Group
Room 201, Home Office
50 Queen Anne's Gate
London SW1H 9AT
Telephone: 0171-273 2084
Fascimile: 0171-222 0211
Internet: http://www.homeoffice.gov.uk/rsd/rsdhome.htm
E-mail: rsd.ho.apollo@gtnet.gov.uk

Occasional Papers can be purchased from:
Home Office
Publications Unit
50 Queen Anne's Gate
London SW1H 9AT
Telephone: 0171-273 2302

HMSO Publications Centre

(Mail, fax and telephone orders only)
PO Box 276, London SW8 5DT
Telephone orders: 0171-873 9090
General enquiries: 0171-873 0011
(queuing system in operation for both numbers)
Fax orders: 0171-873 8200